A Southern Lady's Tea Adventures

Andrea "Andy" McDougal

Published by:

Tea Garden Publications

Case Laminate Edition ISBN 979-8-9987460-5-5
Trade Paper Edition ISBN 979-8-9987460-7-9

Printed on demand in the U.S., the U.K., and Australia For Worldwide Distribution

Dedication

I want to dedicate this book to the people who inspired me, encouraged me to go beyond where I was. Without them, I may never have written this series of tea books. I would never have picked up my tea journey and realized the great adventures I have had along the way.

In 2019, I joined a social media group called Teacups and Cupcakes, and from that point on, I made the most wonderful friends from all over the world, friends who were "lovers of everything tea" and "lovers of everything beautiful." They are the warmest and kindest people to know. This amazing group inspired me in the next two years to understand that I was on a journey that had been filled with the greatest adventures.

This group would not exist were it not for a woman by the name of Diane Sedo. Diane is the Founder and Administrator of this incredible platform that now has more than 27,000 members. Growing up, Diane was given a love and appreciation for everything tea, beginning as a child through visits over the years to different events where tea was served, having her own tea parties in a playhouse built for her by her dad in their backyard and eventually going to tearooms as an adult, joining different tea groups and writing her own very successful and beautiful tea book entitled *Taking Tea with Alice*. So, thank you, Diane, for building a platform that is inviting, warm and endearing to those of us who have come to love and appreciate Teacups and Cupcakes.

I also want to mention the women who so freely encouraged me and inspired me to venture out and accomplish new things I may have never done.

- Linda Schardin Shellabarger, thank you for your continuous words of encouragement for me to step out into uncharted territories and use the gifts that were given to me of an artistic eye for photography and writing that I had only dreamed of doing.
- Jody Benge, thank you for your loving and endearing friendship.
- Jenny Barr in Australia, thank you for your loving friendship and the inspiration from all your teas, recipes for your amazing foods and your heart to serve others.
- Barbara Kirby Davis, you have been an inspiration to me from day one in oh so many ways.
- Janis Parr, a sweet friend and an inspiration to me and many others!
- Sherri House, touching lives through you beautiful tea blog and photography!
- Ann Ginda, wow, your teas, creativity and your heart to make people happy through your incredible teas. You have been an inspiration to me and so many others!
- Char Jorganson, I admire your amazing knowledge and great beauty hosting teas and your incredible collection of Chintz and other beautiful collections.
- William Spaid, you are a great inspiration to me in hosting beautiful teas with beautiful china.
- Janice Van Cleave Rasmussen, Alene Mae, Rett Lew, Bhamini Sudarsanam in India, Andrea Wolford, La Mona Lisa, Betty Menmen, Anna-Mauro Bermudez, Claire Vekony, Ines Emett in Italy, Daniella Kierce in Australia, Sheila Cara Sanford, Debbie McCane, Tracey Lou Dodrill, Shelia Voight, Diane Sterling. And the list goes on and on.

Acknowledgments

I would like to acknowledge the many great men and women of God who have come across my path and brought great adventures into my life, by opening many beautiful doors of ministry to me and allowing me to walk through the gates of many other countries and cultures and to see lives touched and changed for the Kingdom of God.

Contents

Introduction

Welcome to my garden. Won't you come on in.

It's fun, you'll see. We'll have some tea and talk of things to be.

Andrea McDougal

As I look back over the years of my life, I have come to realize that I have had many great adventures. Sometimes we have the tendency to not be aware of how adventurous our lives just may have been. During the time of writing my first tea book, *A Southern Lady's Tea Journey,* I became aware of many things that were left dormant, or maybe simply they were not given enough attention. So they seemed to not have great significance, or the pieces of the puzzle had not all come together yet. So, let's say the pieces of the puzzle have come together.

In my last book, I presented everything in short stories, and so I believe I will continue with that method, but this time I am bringing to you the stories and places over the years of my life that I have enjoyed, unawares, an adventurous tea journey. And I will share with you the places and people I have had the honor to be with and to have enjoyed a cup of tea with, building a path to this book.

You will also be delighted to know that there are recipes for you to use in your own special times of entertaining guests for tea. You will find four wonderful tea friends who are amazing and well-seasoned cooks and tea enthusiasts, who have agreed to share with you some of the best recipes they have to offer.

Since this book will take on an international flare, due to the continued tea journey I have been on for many years now, the recipes and the cooks themselves will have an international flare too. So, about halfway through the book you will find,

my Featured Guests, with some very delicious recipes that will be a delight to your taste buds and beautiful additions to your own tea tables.

A few years ago I had the opportunity to join a wonderful group of "lovers of everything tea" that would share their recipes, photos of the different teas they had hosted and their beautiful china, teapots, teacups and saucers. This group inspired me so much that I began to realize my own tea journey had been taking place for many years, unawares, and has proven to be such a great adventure. Through this group, I have made the best of friends. We have not met face to face yet, because we live all over the United States and in many other countries. Yet, we are so close in friendship of heart that you would think we had known each other for a lifetime.

With the recipes you will find halfway through the book, you will meet a few of the very gifted "lovers of everything tea" and "lovers of everything beautiful" who have made an impact on my life and tea journey. There are so many more of them, with lives so endearing because of their passion and love for everything tea!

So, the journey continues with this *Southern Lady's Tea Adventures.* My first tea book, *A Southern Lady's Tea Journey,* began with the meaning of "journey," and because this part of my journey is about my great tea adventures in other countries, I will prelude everything with What Is an Adventure?

What Is an Adventure?

Life is either a daring adventure or nothing at all

– Helen Keller –

An adventure is something you experience while you are on a journey. You choose to take a step and move forward into uncharted territory. You may not have been cognizant of the fact that you were on a journey. Nor did you realize you were about to have a great adventure ... until you looked back maybe many years after your journey and you thought, "What a great adventure that was!"

Just to live would be an awfully big adventure!

– Peter Pan –

An adventure is an undertaking that could possibly involve danger or unknown risk. It is an exciting and unusual experience. It is a bold and remarkable experience that can lead you to unknown lands, exotic places, joyous and unusual occasions, and your senses will be alerted to things you have never known before, see things your eyes have never seen before, smell fragrances that encapsulate the culture of other lands, and taste the most delicious flavors of tea that have ever glided across your tongue until that moment.

Some journeys take us far from home.
Some adventures lead us to our destiny!

– C.S. Lewis –

I love this quote from C.S. Lewis. For me and for you, our journeys are mingled with unexpected adventures that sometimes just pop up out of nowhere, totally unexpected, a surprise so great that you have to make the decision to say yes, throw every bit of reasoning to the wind, and say, "Why not?" We must see the opportunity for what it truly is: a beautiful gift, not just taking us on a journey, but bringing to us the adventure of a lifetime, leading us into our destiny and purpose. Sometimes you might just stumble into something so unexpected along your journey's path that takes you on the greatest adventures you could ever have imagined could take place in your life.

Would you like an adventure now,
or shall we have our tea first?

– Peter Pan –

The adventure begins with "t"ea.

Adventures are the surprises you get along the journeys of life you have chosen to take!

Andrea McDougal

The adventure is worthwhile in itself.

– Amelia Earhart –t

The Beginnings of a Little Adventurer

And a Cup of "Adventurer's Tea"

As I think back to my childhood adventures, my mind goes back to a sandy area, elevated, in a hilly area of North Louisiana, with water flowing through it. I was with my cousins, the Fluitts, and it was the beginning of many great adventures.

The Indians had made their homes in that area. We could even hear their drums at times, but this particular day we were looking for a treasure I had never known before—Indian arrowheads. It was a cool day, and both the Fluitt family and the Fourroux family (my parents, myself and my constant companion in those days, Lillian) were there together, looking for these stones that had been forged by the Indians of that area from rocks and flints to form the tip of an arrow for hunting wild game. Uncle Jack had the most incredible collection of arrowheads. There was frame after frame with felt backing and glass on top with hundreds of perfectly formed arrowheads, hand-forged by the Indians of those days in Jena, Louisiana.

Looking for arrowheads that day was quiet the adventure. Everything we did when we went to Jena was an adventure to never forget. At Uncle Truman's and Aunt Berta's home, there was a very large worm bed off the very long back porch of their built-by-hand home (built by Uncle Truman, Uncle Jack and my daddy years before). I am still fascinated by this very large worm bed. I had never seen anything like it before and have not seen anything like it since. The men and women of the family who were coffee drinkers or tea drinkers would throw their coffee grounds, used teabags and fruit and vegetable scraps over the banister of the wooden railing of the porch into the rich soil filled with earth worms.

The worms were to be used for fishing and also for the massive vegetable garden. It was such a perfect compost pile, and its soil, along with some of the worms, were put into the garden tended to by Great-Uncle Truman. His very-well-cared-for massive vegetable garden was just a short distance from the porch, and I loved to walk through it because the plants were always taller than I, and the richest colors of green formed an umbrella over my head.

There were many sweet little bunny rabbits in hutches made by Uncle Truman. Lillian and I were each given our own pet rabbit. Daddy built them each a hutch at our home in Slidell, the "little green house," and they would come inside the house at times so that we could play with them.

There was no running water in the house in Jena, but we drew water with a bucket from a beautiful stone well, and the kitchen sink had a hand pump.

Since there was no indoor plumbing, there was an outhouse that we would walk to. To take a bath, we were put into a white porcelain tub in front of the fireplace. This place in Jena was filled with such great adventures.

Mother was a coffee drinker in the mornings, but by afternoon she loved her cup of tea. Great-Aunt Berta would pull down a tin canister filled with loose tea and Mother, Aunt Berta and sometimes Aunt Minnie also would gather around Aunt Berta's very large dining room table for afternoon tea. By this time of day, it usually had a lovely but simple white tablecloth covering the top of it, and there would be biscuits, bacon and maybe an egg or two under the tablecloth waiting for some hungry man or little girl or boy to come along and grab a treat from that morning's breakfast. I can taste the mayhaw jelly even now.

These two and sometimes three ladies would sit there enjoying their afternoon tea. At times it would be taken to the back porch, and they would sit on the rockers and carry on a conversation, but at other times, they just sat there rocking in the old rocking chairs and sipping their hot cups of tea, and at times, coffee. This place in the country was filled with adventures the likes of which this city girl had never known.

A walk through the woods would bring us to the home of Aunt Minnie and Uncle Jack and my Fluitt cousins. Here there would be found even more adventures: giant turtles, mayhaw trees, covered with mayhaw berries (definitely a berry Southern thing). And the outcome from this Southern thing called mayhaws?

Jars and jars filled with the most delicious preserves, jelly or jam that had ever hit my taste buds.

There was the attempted building of forts in the woods. Playing hide and seek, building tents, story-telling and friendships and love that would last a lifetime. This was a place for adventurers. Never a dull or boring moment, always something that a city girl would never otherwise get to experience, unless she had a daddy who was a great adventurer who would take his girls on great adventures.

These great adventures lay at the end of our journey, driving from Slidell or New Orleans as we got older, and the journey there and back was also a beautiful adventure.

Our part of Louisiana was basically as flat as a pancake, but oh my what a beautiful pancake it was. Once we would leave the southern part of Louisiana and head north, there were the most incredible hills. They seemed like mountains to me.

Daddy would drive up to the top of those peaks, and then we would speed down with his foot off the accelerator. I loved it! And the views along the way were so different from our dreamy, architecture and charming homes with gardens and our whimsical life. But, oh how grand it was to go up and down what seemed, to a little girl, to be great mountains and to see beautiful cow pastures and horses and the hills made of red clay and oh so many pine trees and land so beautiful that your eyes would dance with excitement.

There would be many visits over the years of my childhood to this wonderful place and my dearest cousins. Once I had officially joined our families "tea drinking club," whenever I visited this endearing place, I would join the rest of the family in afternoon tea and have a cup of "Adventurer's Tea."

We were created to be happy, to be filled with joy, abounding with fullness of joy, to have a fun-filled life, abounding in strength to experience the journeys of our lives and to have great and unexpected adventures

Andrea McDougal

The thief only comes to steal from you, but I came to give you an abundant life. A life that overflows with life to the fullest.

John 10:10

In the 17th century, tea was introduced into France, but at the first, for medicinal purposes only. Because it was a very costly commodity, it could only be enjoyed by the very wealthy. Therefore, it became a favorite pastime and a daily drink that was enjoyed by the aristocracy of France. These would be the nobles who ruled under their monarchs, the kings and queens.

Until you spread your wings, you'll have no idea how far you can fly.

– Napoleon Bonaparte –

La Fleur De Lis

The French have been tea drinkers for centuries, and they mostly enjoy black tea, but weaker than the usual strong British tea and without milk or lemon.

In the Kitchen Garden at Versailles, the home of Marie Antoinette, was an area where tea was grown for her, and her favorite tea was crafted. To this day, that same tea is still crafted, scented with roses and apples, and is called the Royal Tea of Versailles.

King Louis XVI and Marie Antoinette, the monarchs who later ruled over France, followed suit with lavishly-presented teas and pastries for their court. Their reign would be a short one, and they would be the last monarchs to rule over France.

La Camélia et La Fleur De Lis

King Louis XIV of France began drinking tea for medicinal purposes and then began to indulge in it for its delightful flavors. He drank tea nonstop throughout the days of his reign, and it spread throughout his court. It became an everyday drink that was lavishly rendered with la crème de la crème of the most delectable of pastries.

Along My Journey, a Great Adventure

With a Cup of "Parisian Tea"

"The fragrance of adventure and poetry endlessly pervades each cup of tea."

Henri Mariage

About a year after having my first book, *The Glory of God Revealed*, published, I received a very unexpected phone call from a young lady. The intriguing part of the phone call was the fact that it was coming from Paris, France. I am quite sure it was the first phone call I had ever received from France, much less Paris. I was being summoned, if you will, to be the speaker in a three-day conference. Our conversation was very exciting, the dates were set, and there would be another telephone conversation with the same person confirming our flights and the time of our arrival. I would not meet or talk to the gentleman requesting my appearance until after we arrived in Paris.

As soon as I accepted the invitation, everything was put into motion. In the final conversation I had with this young lady who was making all the arrangements, I was told that we would be staying in Paris for three weeks, and our accommodations and meals would all be provided. What would we do for three weeks in Paris? I had been to other countries before, but I thought I would start here and then introduce you to my other adventures along the journey.

Time flew by quickly, and we were packed and flying to Paris. I would finally meet the young lady who had made all the arrangements for the meetings, and there was a car and driver to chauffeur us to our hotel. Much to my surprise, we were staying at a very beautiful hotel in the most visited region of Paris—Montmartre, French for "the mountain of the martyr"—a beautiful place set on a hill. The meeting would actually be held in a beautiful conference room at the hotel there in Montmartre.

I finally was to meet the people who had read my book and had invited me on this grand adventure. And when I say grand, I mean very grand.

These incredible people were French speaking Africans from the West Coast of that continent. There were those from Cameroon, the Congo and the Ivory Coast. Oh, what beautiful and elegant people, very loving and generous, with charming British accents.

God's ways are most amazing to me. My whole life of ministry has been ... "A people who were not my people became my people."

When I had finished speaking in these awesome meetings, these people had a wonderful going-away party for us, and we were lavished with the most amazing gifts—clothes and jewelry—and some made their gifts. Even children came bringing us beautiful mementos of the days spent with these beautiful people in a most beautiful city that I still have and hold dear to my heart.

When I was not speaking in the conference or in other places besides the meetings at the hotel, we would take many walks. We would walk along the Seine River during the day and even at night.

I am always intrigued with the architecture of houses and neighborhoods, and so all was so beautiful and enchanting to me. We would go to little shops and even were able to go to a little French market that was set up in a large parking lot. There were fruits, vegetables, cooked meat pies and homemade items displayed for sale.

Along our many walks, while we were in Montmartre, my favorite things to encounter were the Trompe L'Oeil paintings on buildings. This is an incredible art form of painting that can incorporate stencils and painting of a scene, and is an art of illusion. These paintings were amazing to me. Some were painted in the most unusual places, on the outside of the tenth story of an apartment complex, for instance. I loved it and to this day would like to do it myself, but definitely not on the outside of a tall building.

Staying at a wonderful hotel in Montmartre, you know that we would have our tea in the morning with our breakfast, with our lunch and also our afternoon tea.

Every cup of tea in Paris was a delight to taste, and everywhere I sat, while I slowly sipped those cups of tea, filled my eyes and heart with sheer joy, charm and whimsy.

Andrea McDougal

After the meetings had ended, we were surprised to know that we were being moved into the center of Paris to stay for the rest of our time in France. Oh, my, this was a place with things I had never encountered before—the Eiffel Tower all the way to the top. What a view! Notre Dame Cathedral, a river cruise along the Seine, the most exquisite Opera House, the Louvre, and yes, I actually saw the real Mona Lisa painting. We would walk everywhere we went. I mostly loved the charming sidewalk cafes and restaurants, with red-checked tablecloths, delicious food, and of course there were many cups of "Paris Tea."

While we were in Paris, it was during one of their worst heat waves, and because it was early spring, the hotels had not yet shifted from heating to air-conditioning. The windows in our room at the hotel were very tall, just as were the windows of all the people across the street from us. Up and down the street, people had their windows open, and men and women would be sitting on their windowsills, looking over the streets full of people shopping, eating, walking, singing, talking and dancing in "a city that never sleeps."

Paris, the city that never sleeps.

In every grand city there are monuments, art galleries, great edifices built by human strength, and what a sight they are to experience firsthand. Then there are the simplest of things, ideals, experiences that may not be so grand in the eyes or hearts of some, but they grant us delightful experiences and leave us all the more touched by their simple beauty and grandeur.

Andrea McDougal

One of my favorite places to visit, besides all the other beautiful places to see in Paris, was to see the people selling artwork, French advertisement posters, books and stamps and many other fun things, out of their big wooden boxes and stands that were painted green. These were known as the Bouquinistes of Paris. I was there, amidst the wonderful green boxes we had only seen in movies, like the 1963 Charade movie with Cary Grant and Audrey Hepburn. I was elated to be there and to bring home some beautiful pieces of advertisement posters to give as gifts and to grace the walls of my home.

Big wooden boxes and stands that were painted green, the Bouquinistes of Paris. These wonderful green boxes and stands were first established in Paris in the 16th century and continue today along the River Seine. Selling artwork, prints, French advertisements, books and stamps. Bouquinistes means "little book."

Andrea McDougal

Another very simple thing I loved to do in Paris was when we would stop for tea or to eat a meal, and that is exactly what we did after our shopping spree among the green boxes and stands. I loved to see the walls of the French cafes and restaurants graced in beautiful, gold filigree frames, filled with delightful, vintage postcards. All were so beautifully created, sheer perfection of tiny pieces of art. I longed to own them and to be able to take them home with me. They were so beautiful and whimsical. There were several cards to each golden frame. I loved them so. And then to sit in one of these dreamy and whimsy-filled French eateries with the most delectable flavors to enter my mouth and red-checkered tablecloths and curtains and slowly sip cup after cup of wonderful "Parisian tea."

I love Paris in the springtime.

31

Tea in London with A. A. Milne

With a cup of "Winnie the Pooh Tea""

A.A. Milne, or Alan Alexander Milne, was the author of the wonderful books about a bear by the name of Winnie the Pooh and his dear companion, Piglet. Milne was born in London and lived in Great Britain his whole life.
I think he was a genius with a very big heart!
Following are quotes that he wrote about tea, but Winnie the Pooh and sometimes Piglet actually spoke them.

"I don't feel much like Pooh today," said Pooh.
"There, there," said Piglet
"I'll bring you tea and honey until you do."

"Tea and honey is a Very Grand Thing."

"A Proper Tea is much nicer than a
Very Nearly Tea,
Which is one you forget about afterwards."

"Christopher Robin was home by this time, because it was the afternoon, and he was so glad to see them that they stayed there until very nearly tea-time, and then they had a Very Nearly Tea, which is one you forget about afterwards and hurried on to Pooh Corner, so as to see Eeyore before it was too late to have a Proper Tea with Owl."

What is a Very Nearly Tea as compared to a Proper Tea?

A Very Nearly Tea is a cup of tea you fix in a hurry, you drink it down quickly, and you forget everything about it. But a Proper Tea is the kind of tea that you invite a friend over or you sit down with someone special and you offer them a slice of Honey Cake, or a Scottish Cookie or a Meringue Drop Cookie, and it is never forgotten! Now that is a Proper Tea.

Another Great Adventure
"I Am Going to See the Queen"
And to Drink Many Cups of "Royal Tea"

Our time in Paris had not come to an end. There was still another week left for us before we would have to make our way home to the US. Someone had a most incredible idea, and that was for us to take a train to London. Now, this was not an ordinary train; this was the Bullet. The Bullet would travel on land and race through one of the most famous underwater tunnels in the world. It would travel at the top speed of 320 km/h or, in US miles, 200 mph, and would travel 344 km or 214 miles in a bit over two hours.

We left most of our luggage and belongings, packed for our return home, with our host. I was on a journey, the journey of lifetime, and yet the greatest adventures had come to wrap itself around me and take me along and carry me on the wind of the Spirit of God, who was lavishing me with the most beautiful gifts for my eyes to behold!

The land we traveled over was beautiful and pastoral. Then under the sea we went, and when our journey was nearing its end, the Bullet took us out from the tunnel in the deep, and the sight my eyes beheld took my breath away. There, before us, were the beautiful and awe-inspiring white cliffs of Dover. To some that might not seem eventful, but for me it was a grand sight that will never leave me. It was a beautiful gift to me along this great adventure I was placed upon, leading me to my destiny.

Fortunately for us, the Bullet went straight to Waterloo Station, and when we went out, a little weary and imagining a long walk to find a hotel, I was surprises to find that we were in the heart of London, and only a block or two away was a wonderful hotel for us to stay in.

I have often thought that I would like to take the Queen to afternoon tea.

Andrea McDougal

Our hotel stay was perfect, and I enjoyed our breakfasts. Breakfast was oh so delicious and very British. Seating in the dining room gave us a perfect view of a glassed-in area of the gift shop, and there, lined up so perfectly and on glass shelves, was a vast array of every kind of Sadler Teapot. Oh, my, they were so beautiful, so pleasing to the eyes! Displayed in all their glory with brilliant colors, shapes and sizes, a delight to my senses.

Our tea, as you can imagine, was delicious.
There were cups of English Breakfast,
Earl Grey with the fragrance of bergamot,
a very fragrant Darjeeling with a distinctive muscatel aroma
and Lady Grey with its hint of citrus.

We were right around the corner from the River Thames. Just a short walk of a few feet, and there was the river before us with the Eye of London, the most massive and amazingly gigantic Ferris wheel you could ever see. Each compartment for people to get into and take a ride holds 28, and it moves so slowly you could not see it move from the ground. Being in it, you had a 360° view, seeing every iconic sight of London for miles. It was truly most appropriately named The Eye of London.

Right across the River Thames from our hotel was Big Ben, the House of Parliament, Bird Cage Walk, Buckingham Palace, Westminster Abbey, Tower Bridge, the Tower of London and #10 Downing Street. History was right before us, surrounding us within feet of where we were staying. I felt like a little child who had just been given the most amazing gifts.

My grandmother you met in my first book, *A Southern Lady's Tea Journey*, lived in England for several years, and now I was walking the streets and seeing the sights she had enjoyed during her time there. Every step we took filled my eyes with amazement, that I was in a place I could have only dreamed to one day be.

Sereni-tea

Noun: the absence of stress while drinking tea.

I so loved strolling along beautiful Bird Cage Walk. I thought it to be a very charming name, along with the other walks and street names. The name came into being because of King James I, who had a particular penchant for exotic birds and kept many of them in cages and aviaries lining this street. Thus the name Bird Cage Walk. The walkway led us through a beautiful park and on to Buckingham Palace.

As we stood in front of the gates to the palace, they opened, and a convertible sports car passed in front of us with one of the princes of the royal family. Buckingham Palace Road led us in front of the Queen's equestrian stables. We were able to see the horses being prepared for the Queen's Official Birthday Parade, known as Trooping the Colour.

We were also given a view of Queen Elizabeth as she was out promoting tourism. Of course, a hat was donning her head, and her traditional gloves and purse were in hand.

I loved all the amazing tours we took—to Westminster Abbey and the Tower of London—and learning the fate of many of the royals, including Mary, Queen of Scots, seeing the Crown Jewels and all the other beautiful sights and sounds.

In England, everything stops for tea.

There is nothing more wonderfully elegant than dressing and arriving at a magnificent tearoom. They were created by royalty. And the reason for it is that it was a drink that only the aristocrats, who were the nobles under the monarchs, could afford. Tea was a commodity that was so expensive, traveling from distant places such as China or India or other distant and foreign lands.

To walk into a grand tearoom, see the décor, be seated and have afternoon tea definitely makes you feel like royalty. It is an experience you cannot find just anywhere. It is grand in all aspects.

Andrea McDougal

There is a lovely tearoom at Kensington Palace called the Kensington Palace Pavilion Tea Room. It is the only place in town where you can enjoy a traditional afternoon tea on the grounds of a royal palace, and you will be amidst 300 years of royal history. It is a glorious affair that one should not miss.

Our walks would always open up to us such beauty and historical places, like the Prime Minister's housing at #10 Downing Street. The day we went to Kensington was a spur-of-the-moment decision, and we walked and ran to get to the gates before they closed. I have to say I thoroughly loved visiting Kensington Palace, the home of Princess Diana and of many other world-famous royals. The apartments, the exquisite furnishings, the tapestries ... everything done in grand style, the grounds and gardens done with sheer perfection, and a beautiful gift shop with charming gifts and such an amazingly beautiful tearoom!

Sir Thomas Lipton

and Lipton Tea

Perhaps no one has done more to promote tea than the Scottish merchandising whiz Sir Thomas Lipton. After the coffee blight of the mid-1880s decimated the coffee crops in Ceylon, Lipton purchased bankrupt estates in Ceylon and began cultivating tea. He undercut the going selling price for tea and created the slogan "Direct from the Tea Gardens to the Teapot," a selling tactic that brought him great financial success. Lipton emphasized the adventurous nature of his tea enterprise and played on the exotic, foreign nature of Ceylon to captivate the interest of tea drinkers back home.

Lipton was the first merchant to sell his tea in sealed packets, emphasizing freshness, cleanliness, and honest weight. He became a millionaire and succeeded by capturing the loyalty of tea drinkers in both England and later in America. His efforts to encourage and realize colonial tea expansion in Ceylon added to the British Empire's already firmly established control of tea production in India. This expansion brought about the ability of the British to control tea cultivation at the source and to sever trade ties with China for tea forever.

On Our Way to Glasgow
With Tiny Pots of "Scottish Black Tea"

Because we were in London at the time of the Queen's birthday, I am sure you would speculate that we were able to attend. But we were not. Our time was running short, and within a few days we would have to be back in Paris. We vacillated a little on what we should do. I had been to Amsterdam a few years before on a prior trip to Israel, and Amsterdam is one of my favorite places to visit. I love the delft blue and white china that my grandmother gave me a love for. I had read that we could take a ferry from England across the North Sea to Amsterdam, but it would take 24 hours to get there and 24 hours to get back. As adventurous as it would have been, someone had a much better idea. We rented a car in London (which was hysterical at times because we were totally discombobulated driving on the wrong side of the road and on the wrong side of the car).

After leaving London and then England itself, we were on a motorway in Scotland heading for Glasgow. The motorways in Great Britain are nothing like our interstates, that are littered with billboards and signs for everything imaginable, including roads, exits, highways and cities. The motorway we were on was one way, and in between the two different directions of flowing traffic was a median with trees.

The gas stations, or what we might consider to be a convenience store, were all obscure and hidden for the most part behind trees, and you could only notice them as you were approaching their area. We had been driving for some time and needed a little pick-me-up to continue our journey on to Glasgow for the night. We were not in need of gasoline, only something to drink or a snack to take with us.

As we walked into what we thought was a convenience store, there was a very large room filled with many tables and chairs, and everyone there seem to be drinking hot tea. So, we proceeded to do what everyone else was doing. We sat down at one of the tables and placed our order for hot tea, "Scottish black tea," if you please, and we ordered a scone to share. What we had expected to be a convenience store was actually a convenience tearoom, definitely not fancy, but all the same, very refreshing.

I am sure that you well-versed tea lovers and tea drinkers have already experienced this in your life, but this little lady from the Deep South had not yet experienced this simple but wonderful little treat. When our tea was brought to us, of course, we had our cups and tea bags, but our hot water was brought to us in the cutest little stainless teapots. I am sure you can tell that it is in the smallest of things that I receive so much joy and delight.

I was so enamored with this unexpected treat, tiny teapots from which to pour our hot water into our teacups. This, of course, was some years ago, and now in our own society and restaurants, when you ask for a cup of hot tea, you are brought the same type of small stainless teapot brimming with hot water. The scone, of course, was delicious, and we were glad we shared it, and, with it, our many cups of "Scottish black tea."

Before we arrived in Glasgow, we experienced many roundabouts while we were driving. It really started out to be very much fun, with a lot of laughter. Round-abouts were not that popular in the U.S. at the time, but it seems now, years later, they are popping up in the most unlikely places. They are everywhere, which does make for a faster flow of traffic.

The sun was setting, and night was quickly approaching. If you will remember, I mentioned the signs not being very prolific on the motorways. All of that, including the roundabouts (that at first were so much fun, simply because we had to keep going around and around them to find which exit we were to take to get off the roundabout to find our hotel in time to check in). As we went around and around in the roundabouts, laughter filled the car, but the later it became, the more the laughter diminished, as fatigue began to set in. Oh my goodness, please get us to our hotel in Glasgow. We made it, obviously.

Everything in Glasgow was wonderful and filled with history and, yes, tearooms. The next morning our next adventure was calling us, and so we had our Scottish breakfast with our cups of "Scottish black tea" and then headed off to our next adventure.

On Our Way to Oban on the Sea

The McDougal Castle and Cups of "McDougal Tea"

Oh, ye'll take the high road and I'll take the low road, and I'll be in Scotland afore ye.

Where me and my true love will never meet again,

On the bonnie, bonnie banks of Loch Lomond.

Our drive from Glasgow to Oban was most incredible! This pathway we were on had been traveled upon by the peoples of Scotland and those who traveled to see and experience such beauty for many, many years. It is known as the Western Highlands of Scotland, and the scenery was breathtaking. Just to see the famous loches (lakes) is a sight you can never forget. For instance, the well-known Loch Lomond that we have sung about from the time we were small children. "The Bonnie Banks of Loch Lomond" did take my breath away. All the different shades of green ... the loches themselves with such a rich color of blue, and then there were the small mountains or hilly cliffs that would jet straight up out of the water. It was not in a gradual way, with land or beach around them, but simply straight up out of the water as if to say, "Here I am in all my strength and beauty."

After about a two-hour drive from Glasgow, we arrived at beautiful Oban. I instantly fell in love with Oban, and it remains in my heart even to this day. It is a very picturesque seaside town, known as the jewel in the starry crown of Argyll and Bute. Oban sits on the dark blue waters of the Firth of Lorn. I remember thinking that every direction I would turn, my eyes were filled with the beauty and charm of what I call Oban on the Sea.

Our first stop was at the McDougal Castle, and it was my first ever castle to see or to enter. It is a ruin now that stands quite tall and is still intact with its stairs of stone, individual rooms and floor levels. It is, to this day, in the care of the leader of the McDougal Clan. In each clan, the clan brooch is handed down from generation to generation to the clan leader, heir to or the head of the clan. Today the McDougal Clan leader just so happens to be a woman. The brooch is worn at the shoulder, at the top of the clan's tartan scarf.

Next, of course, we began to visit all the charming gift shops and to see all the sites that we could see. Every little gift shop was filled with every imaginable Scottish mug and souvenir. And then our eyes beheld everything McDougal. In downtown Oban was a very large merchant store called McDougal's General Store. In this store was a multitude of McDougal products, grocery items and everything imaginable, even ice cream. I purchased three bags of McDougal Flour—self-rising, sponge flour and regular flour—which were all wonderful. But my greatest find in Oban, Scotland was a Sadler tea canister with aristocratic nobles having afternoon tea. To this day, it sits prominently on a beautiful marble-topped nightstand in our bedroom.

Before our journey on to the next place in Scotland, we sat in a charming place eating a large open-faced scone topped with a delicious stew. As we looked out of the sweet little eatery, we could see the beautiful masses of large boats, shipping vessels, and personal boats of different kinds, that were docked in the Bay of Oban and at other land masses nearby. I remember thinking that if we were to continue south from there, we would find ourselves in Wales.

During our time in Oban and all of Scotland, it was very cold, and we welcomed our cups of tea to keep us warm. We drank what seemed to be a black chai tea, but we were assured it was not a chai. Yet, our cups of a rich black tea had the taste of cinnamon and nutmeg. We loved the taste and the warmth if brought to our chilled bodies, and we drank several cups of "McDougal Tea."

There is nothing more delightful on a cold day than a warm scone and a cup of "McDougal Tea."

Stonehaven on the North Sea

A Place Where the Sun Never Set, and the "Stonehaven Tea" and "North Sea Tea" Were Oh So Wonderful!

On our way to the eastern edge of Scotland, there were things for us to see. We went to the church and town of Inverarity, Scotland, where some of our other family members hailed from, and it has been a family name through many generations. Also, one of the greatest revivals to hit Scotland was in that area, besides the many great awakenings over the years in all of Scotland.

We visited Sterling Castle, which was most magnificent and historical. King James I, who had the King James Bible put into print, was the King of Scotland and lived at Sterling Castle before he became the King of England and Scotland. One of the first King James Bibles that was put into print was at Sterling, and we were able to have a glance at it. Mary, Queen of the Scots, also made her residence there for a short period of time. Many royals would make their way to Sterling, to stay or to live, because it was such a lavish and beautiful place to visit or to stay for periods of time. There is a very large meeting hall that was used for receiving and entertaining royalty, but on Sundays it became a church.

When leaving the castle that was quite grand and spread out over many acres of land, to its right was a very large and beautiful grassy area with a monument to the beloved Sir William Wallace, known to many as Braveheart.

At the closing of the day, we found ourselves on the North Sea. Little did we know that the sun would hardly set in the quaintest of villages called Stonehaven. In fact, by 5 am the next day, the sun had just begun to set and would vaguely disappear for a couple of hours. What a dreamy and unforgettable village we would be staying in! Before finding a place to stay, we walked along a wall that was built to hold back the sea from destroying the beautiful harbor and village.

We were able to find a quaint little B&B owned by a man who did the most incredible inlaid pieces of furniture, boxes and wooden bracelets. We arrived that evening just in time for everyone to be going to bed, and yet the sun was out brightly.

When we went down to see our host the next morning, he had prepared a most delicious and hearty breakfast for us to enjoy. I watched as he took great care in making our tea. He had already heated a kettle of water hanging over his fireplace. He poured the water into his Stewart Clan teapot and placed the precise amount of loose-leaf tea into his pot. He let the tea steep, then placed lovely tea strainers over our teacups and poured the hot tea into them. It was his own blend that he called Stonehaven Tea. It was absolutely a most delightful time, as we sat there and enjoyed our breakfast, with freshly-baked scones, eggs, ham and a delicious hash, and we enjoyed many cups of Stonehaven Tea.

Our host spoke to us proudly and with tears of how the Americans came to the rescue of Europe and drove back the forces of evil at the hands of Hitler. He made known his great gratitude to our country and the American Forces that saved Europe and the world. Our time spent with him was such a warm and endearing one that we hated to leave, but we knew that we had to be leaving, for we still had a journey before us and would have to get to London, take the Bullet back to Paris, retrieve our luggage and catch our flight back to the States.

Before we left, our host gave me a beautiful gift, a wooden bracelet he had made from a dark wood with lighter shades of inlaid wood around it. I still have that prized possession, and you may spot it in one of the Scottish photos.

The many cups of "Stonehaven Tea" we were served in his Stewart Clan teacups energized us for our journey from the northern part of Scotland just below the city of Aberdeen, all the way along the coast of the North Sea, through many hilly villages to our right and the constant North Sea to our left. We stopped along the way to visit a castle positioned on a high place overlooking the North Sea. Our next stop was St. Andrews, where we saw the world famous St. Andrews Golf Course. We visited the church, now just a shell, which was the birthplace of the Scottish Reformation in 1560: "The just shall live by faith and not by works,"

As we walked along in front of St. Andrews University, we happened upon a traditional Scottish wedding with bagpipes and the men dressed in the traditional tartan kilts and garb.

We then drove on to Edinburgh University, opened in 1583 and still one of the most prestigious and oldest universities in the English-speaking world. Before leaving the area, we enjoyed another cup of "North Sea Tea."

Beautiful Gretna Green

Because of the strict marriage laws in England, many couples would leave England and head straight for Gretna Green and there make their vows, seal their marriage and head back into England as man and wife. Thus, Gretna Green is famous for runaway marriages.

Our great adventure was coming to an end. It had begun in Paris and then on to London and all throughout Scotland. Our travels had brought us through beautiful Scotland and many places of enjoying and having tea and scones and delicious Scottish foods, but our time was fast running out. Very soon, we must be heading back home, to the U.S. There was so much history, beauty and fun that had been taken in that now it would only be memories.

Memories that would be hid for a lifetime in our hearts and minds of such a great adventure!

Andrea McDougal

Before we crossed the border from Scotland back into England, we decided to make one last stop, at Gretna Green. Here I found such great mementos to bring back home to family, sisters, mother, daughters, grandchildren and friends. The item I loved the most was a beautiful miniature teapot that you will find on the opposite page. It came in a wonderful and very sturdy gift box that was lined in satin that caressed the delicate and very beautiful bone china teapot. To this day it remains a most favorite teapot that sits prominently with the Sadler Afternoon Tea Caddy I bought at the McDougal General Store in Oban on the Sea on my marble-top nightstand.

Life is like a cup of tea to be filled to the brim and enjoyed with friends and family!

Our journey, that had been filled with great adventures, was coming to an end. It would now take us back to London, to catch the Bullet, leaving the white cliffs of Dover behind, traveling under the English Channel through a tunnel and back to Paris to get our luggage and return to our lives in Louisiana.

As soon as I saw you, I knew a grand adventure was about to happen.

– Winnie the Pooh–

The Greatest Adventures in Mexico

And a Cup of "Lemon Grass Tea"

My first international adventure was to Guadalajara, Mexico. We traveled there in 1986 to do missionary work. My adventures of being a missionary must go into another book, one that will be filled with many salvations, miracles, signs and wonders. But for this book, many of my great adventures will be brief so as to focus on tea.

I will say this: it was quite an adventure. The sights, the sounds, the architecture, the beautiful people, the food ... it was all oh so delicious, historical, a magnificent city! It was another world that I loved so very much.

We traveled to the surrounding mountainous areas, very treacherous places where the people still used horses and mules for travel and lived lives from a prior century. I must say that I loved the artisan work all throughout Mexico—the pottery, glass, metal and iron work.

In 1989, we found ourselves leaving our home and moving outside of Juarez, Mexico, which I absolutely loved! It was just myself and my husband and our six-year-old daughter, Elizabeth. My other three children were older and remained in Baton Rouge. My oldest son, Patrick, was in the Army and was stationed in Germany. He soon came for a visit and brought us to meet his family, two of our newest grandchildren, Little Pat and Jennifer. Be still my heart! We were far from home, so to see my oldest son and his precious family made me so very happy.

Prior to Patrick bringing his family for us to meet, my eldest daughter, Kimberly, and my first-born grandchild, Amy, and our youngest son, Kenny, flew out to be with us. Each visit was so wonderful for me, but the parting was much too difficult.

Our work in the Juarez area was incredible. We started three churches, one in Zaragoza, where the people moved in from the interior of Mexico to get jobs at the Twin Plants (American companies located at the border of Juarez). These people literally lived in cardboard boxes they put together with bottle caps and nails. The other church was to the west of Juarez, in Anapra, right close to a garbage dump. We also started a church in El Paso, Texas.

We had the greatest of times in Mexico. Brother Jose Sanchez, after every service, would prepare us wonderful meals, especially at Christmas. It was quite the banquet. After the services in the winter, Brother Jose would send his son, Angel, down the dirt road, and he would come back with something we had never tasted before in the area of tea. Angel returned with a large bunch of what looked like long grass. Brother Jose was so happy when he brought out the hot cups of tea. It was such a very cold night. He said to me, "This is special for you. Do you know what this is?" Of course, I didn't. I took a sip, and it was delicious. He had sweetened it just right, with fresh honey from the comb. He was so proud of the cup of tea he gave me. He declared, "This is lemon grass tea! This is good for you. Can you taste the lemon?" This dear man of God, a dear, dear friend, living in the desert with hardly anything to his name, thus introduced me to a delicious cup of tea. He treated me like a queen, and his heart was filled with joy. I have loved "Lemon Grass Tea" ever since.

Tea in Israel

The national tea in Israel is a Wissotzky tea bag containing mint "nana," which is similar to a Moroccan tea. But there is a difference between the Israeli and a true Moroccan tea, which is made with Chinese green tea with mint leaves added.

Tea is extremely popular in Israel with tearooms and teashops all over the country. The most popular teas are lemon verbena and fruit-based infusions. But, they also go according to the diversity of individual taste buds.

Come, let us have some tea and continue to talk about happy things.

– Rabbi Chaim Potok –

Everywhere we went in Israel, from Tel Aviv to Jerusalem, to the Dead Sea and north to the Sea of Galilee, on the northern shore by Tabgha, and down the western shore to Tiberias and westward to Haifa, and on to Tel Aviv, I always had the most delicious cups of tea, rich and full of flavor, sweetened with a fresh raw honey and sometimes a sprig of mint.
Andrea McDougal

The Tea Adventure of a Lifetime–Amsterdam and Israel

Those who go down to the sea and do business in deep waters, they shall see the wonders of God. – Psalm 107:23-24

Just a couple of weeks before my next adventure, I had ordered a couple of books for my youngest daughter, Elizabeth. One was *The Diary of Anne Frank,* and the other was also a book about her life. As we sat there looking through the books, I said to her. "Wouldn't it be wonderful if we got to go to Amsterdam to visit the house where Ann Frank lived." She replied, "No, Momma, you will go there first, and you will tell me all about it." Little did I know that in just a couple of weeks I would be in a place that I could have never imagined I would be.

Within twenty-four hours, on a very hot and sweltering summer day along the Gulf Coast of Mississippi, I would truly stumble into my next great adventure. I was locked out of my room, late for a meeting and had to walk for what seemed a couple of blocks in very hot and humid conditions to get to the conference center. There was a woman ministering whom I had met before, and every time I was in her presence, things would be put into motion in my life, and I would have an encounter with God.

For those of you who may know her, it was Ruth Ward Heflin. We practically stumbled into each other that day, she began to speak over my life, and the next thing I knew, just two weeks later, I was in her home in Jerusalem for the Feast of Tabernacles celebration. It was one of the most amazing experiences, to be at the Wailing Wall in the Old City of Jerusalem and see the masses of Hasidic Jews blowing their shofars and celebrating Succot.

But first, I must introduce a dear friend, Victoria Comeaux. It turned out that Victoria was very much desirous of us going to Israel together. There are so many more details to this amazing story of such miracles, wonders and glory that it can only be told in another book. Again, this book must be restricted to tea adventures. This was an adventure that changed my life and ministry forever.

It would be just Victoria and myself going to Israel, but first we had a short layover in a city that I love, Amsterdam. We took a train from the airport and very shortly arrived in Amsterdam. There we visited an emporium for Delft China. There were blue and white teapots, dishes, teacups and saucers, beautiful Dutch figurines, anything you could imagine for your tea table. As you can imagine, we shopped.

We visited the home of Anne Frank, the place my youngest daughter and I had talked about going to just a couple of weeks before, not knowing that I would actually be there. What a beautiful and enchanting place it was! I loved the shops and the sites. I have been back to Amsterdam two more times since then.

We took the train back to the airport, retrieved our luggage and were now on to our next stop. The next flight landed in Tel Aviv. After spending the night there, we rented a car and drove straight to Jerusalem.

I could not have asked for a better traveling companion. Victoria was so creative and knowledgeable, and she made sure we went to the most amazing places in our great adventure.

The very first place we stopped to celebrate this great adventure was to have tea at the Crown Plaza. My first thought was, "I am not dressed nice enough to have tea in this beautiful dining/tearoom," but we were there, so we did it. We lifted our cups to each other, being thankful to be around the world on such a great adventure.

We would then find ourselves in the most beautiful, historical and fascinating places of the area. We drank tea at a wonderful café on the third floor of a building in the Old City. Looking to my left was the Wailing Wall, and looking straight ahead was the golden dome on the Temple Mount. The sights, the sounds ... everything was most incredible!

We found ourselves on what is called the Via Dolorosa, and as we passed a little shop, a young man kept inviting us to go into his store. His English was very poor, but he was insisting that we go in. He wanted to show us something and to offer us some Turkish Tea. I was apprehensive. As we went in, I was thinking, "We should not be doing this." He began to say, in very broken English, "You come here. I want to show you something." We followed him down some carved-out stone stairs to another level under his store. I was thinking we are about to be killed, and my husband and family would never know what happened to me.

We arrived safely at what he had wanted us to see. It was the original pavement of the Via Dolorosa "the way of pain and sorrow," "the way of the cross," the street where Jesus carried His cross for you and me. We were so touched to be standing on such hallowed ground. Our guide did not forget that he had offered us some Turkish tea, and he served us each a cup to take with us on our journey.

We would be staying at Ruth Ward Heflin's home on Mount Zion, and there many cups of hot tea would be served to us. I offered to fix Ruth some tea and bring it to her, just so I could lovingly serve her, but she told me that her faithful companion, Connie, knew exactly how she liked her tea and would bring it to her tea in her room.

We ate the grandest meals at Ruth's home. The most wonderful times were when we would eat outside under a very large pergola covered with grape vines to shade us from the sun. Her cook for many years would prepare meals for dignitaries who would travel from all over the world to visit Ruth and be in her services and, if they were fortunate enough, dine at her table.

This particular day would be no different. The food was delectable, and the company was grand. There were people there who had traveled from near and far to be with Ruth, especially during the Feast of Tabernacles. The gentleman I had the honor to sit next to was an ambassador from West Africa. There was a large group of us sitting under the pergola, and the first thing to be served was our cups of tea. I enjoyed speaking with the ambassador about his travels and his country.

Afterward, we were able to experience the very elaborate Feast of Tabernacles. It was amazingly beautiful, with dancers and music and great productions. We would then leave Ruth's and begin to head north to the Sea of Galilee. We went to the Mount of Beatitudes and visited Tabgha where the loves and fishes were multiplied to feed the thousands who followed Jesus to hear His teachings.

Just across from Tabgha, we noticed, as we were leaving, a very beautiful area with a church way to the back of a lush property that was gated. We got out of the car to have a look at what was before us. Victoria and I were very intrigued with what we were seeing, and before we knew it, a young man, dressed in a long brown robe, was heading toward the gate where we were standing. He was a monk who had been given the care of this great property on the edge of the Sea of Galilee that housed a very old church. He unlocked the gate and asked us to come in.

He explained that he was the caretaker of the church and that it was being completely restored. As he began to show us around inside, he took us to the most beautiful paintings of each of the individual saints. The créme de la créme of artists had been hired from all over the world, but mostly Italy, and sent there to completely restore the aged and decaying paintings throughout the church. It was a most beautiful and tedious undertaking, but little by little was being accomplished. My favorite among the paintings was of Joan of Arc.

After our tour of the church, he brought us to a very large veranda attached to the back of the church. It was beautiful to look out over the Sea of Galilee from there. He offered us a cup of tea and soon brought it and served us on the veranda. As we sat there, the sun was beginning to set, but we were enjoying our cup of "Galilee Tea."

Later, we would meet a little Bedouin man at the Dead Sea, who also offered us a cup of tea. We would have tea on the Sea of Galilee, and one of my favorite places was in the city of Tiberias, a beautiful hilly area on the western shore of the Sea of Galilee. As we sat there drinking our tea at a very lovely restaurant, we could see out over the whole Sea of Galilee.

There were so many more wonderful things we experienced on this trip, but then our trip had to come to an end. We would soon be flying back home. Two days later, I would be flying into Kingston, Jamaica, where I would be speaking in some meetings. I thought the meetings would be in Kingston, but as it turned out, they were to be held in beautiful Ochoa Rios, Eight Rivers, on the northern coast of Jamaica. My dear friend and companion, Victoria, would be traveling with me once again.

So many great adventures took place on the trip to Israel, and each adventure was filled with many great miracles and destiny for my life that they simply cannot be put into this little book about tea. But the wonderful things—the adventures, the miracles, signs and wonders that took place—can be found for you to read in my books *His Wonders in the Deep, The Glory of God Revealed* and *Your Camels Are Coming*.

I began this book with a quote from C.S. Lewis that puts this all into perspective, and I will place it here again, for it seems so apropos:

"Some journeys take us far from home.
Some adventures lead us to our destiny."
– C.S. Lewis –

I would travel to Israel three more times, once with Robert Sterns' Ministry, another time I took a group of men and women in my ministry, and the last trip I was invited to be the speaker in a Glory Conference in the Old City of Jerusalem. I look forward to another soon return!

The Dutch Are Lovers of Tea and Chocolate

Just flying into the airports of Holland, you will become profoundly aware firsthand that the Dutch are not only lovers of tea, but also lovers of the most delicious chocolates! For me, the two go hand and hand with each other!

Have you ever had a cup of tea flavored with chocolate? It is most delicious! You can pour liquid chocolate into a cup of hot tea or sprinkle chocolate nibs or chips into a hot cup of your favorite tea, and even top it off with clotted cream or a more conventional type of cream—a whipped cream. It is all delicious, no matter how you chose to fix it. And if you have never tasted Dutch chocolates, you are in for a real treat!

Most European breakfasts are laced with chocolate, Nutella, chocolate bars, chips that are spooned onto your plate or into your hot cup of tea or even coffee, should you so desire. It is believed that all breakfasts should begin with, not only your standard breakfast menu, but also with chocolate. And let's not forget a steeping pot of tea and a sweet biscuit/cookie or two.

We also loved our visits to the beautiful pastry shops and the most incredible bread stores, and of course, the Delft pottery stores and lovely tearooms.

Tea in Holland

The Dutch use no milk with their tea, but add lots of flavor to it. Because their preferred tea is flavored, those teas do not lend themselves to being served with milk. And so the Dutch never acquired a taste for a milky tea, like the British did.

The Dutch never use the term "cuppa" as the British do. They usually have some "thee" [a French word pronounced "tay"]. In the history of tea consumption by the Dutch, it was originally cha.

Orange Pekoe Tea has its origins with the Dutch and carries the connotation of being "Royal Tea."

Amsterdam, Lagos, Freetown and Haarlem

And Cups of "Nigerian Tea" and "Old Country Rose Tea"

In a small country in West Africa, Sierra Leon (Lion Mountain), a Bible school was started in 1986 in the capital city, Freetown. There would be 20 students who graduated from that first class. One of those students was a young man by the name of Desmond Thomas, and Desmond continued his life in full-time ministry. Twenty years later, we received a phone call from him, saying that he had once again raised up a Bible School in Freetown and he wanted to invite us to the graduation of more than 60 students. Thus, began a beautiful journey filled with great adventures!

Once Again, in Amsterdam

Our first stop would once again be Amsterdam, one of my favorite cities to visit. But this time our layover would be for several days, and we would get to experience more of this very whimsical and magical city. I made all our arrangements before we left home, and we were able to catch a train from the airport into Amsterdam and go directly to a very charming bed-and-breakfast-like hotel. Our room was on the fourth floor, and the stairs to get up there were quite narrow and steep. The best part of our stay at the B&B, as always, was the delicious European-style breakfasts, which, just about anywhere in Europe, along with your choice of coffee or tea, included some type of chocolate, yogurts, rich breads, eggs and a meat, and sometimes either fruit or slices of tomato and possibly olives.

The whole of Amsterdam is built with canals instead of streets and with walkways to the right and the left of the waterways. Because their streets are beautiful canals, there are fewer cars, but bicycles by the thousands. Basically, everyone did their commuting to anywhere in the city on bicycle. It was wonderful and a beautiful sight!

Tea in Lagos, Nigeria

Tea in Lagos, Nigeria is a daily adventure, whether you are taking a cup of tea with a friend as a visitor, in the privacy of your own home or on the streets of Lagos, stopping at the vendors along the side of the road. It is a drink of choice for the peoples of Lagos and all throughout Nigeria.

Many things have changed in Lagos and the rest of Nigeria over the years. There has been a rise in fast-food shops and among these makeshift shops or stands, along the roadside, there is the seller of tea.

Who or what is "the seller of tea"? They are usually known as or referred to as Mai Shai, a "brewer of tea" in Hausa, meaning a class of people among the ruling class, with their own language and culture.

Now this is a very important place of meeting, for it is where many gather very early in the morning until late in the evening, to take a cup of tea.

Much business is transpired, communication takes place, and friendships are built in these moments shared at the makeshift buildings operated by the seller or brewer of tea.

Whether it is for a morning cup of tea, afternoon tea, evening tea or a cup of herbs to help with sleep, these stands have grown in popularity.

The Tea Room Lagos

There are also tea rooms in Lagos and other parts of Nigeria that are very elegant and beautiful. They promise to usher you into a magical place filled with floristry, culinary delights and the best teas the world has to offer. One is known as The Tea Room Lagos.
The color palette, in itself, is a soothing delight to the eyes, with pastels, mauves and pinks. Exquisite chandeliers are dripping with large bouquets of flowers.

On to Nigeria for Another Great Adventure

And Cups of "Nigerian Tea"

Fortunately, I had made our travel plans for Nigeria way in advance. I was able to contact a wonderful organization and communicate with the head of The Bible Society of Nigeria to see if they could recommend housing for us. Much to my surprise, they had housing on the Bible Society compound and welcomed us to stay there.

Our plane would arrive late in the evening in Lagos, the capital. The cab drivers and bus drivers would stand outside the glassed windows and doors of the airport, and it was best that the airplane passengers, such as ourselves, would not go out the doors of the airport, especially if we were not nationals. So there we stood, late at night, looking for some sign from our host, letting us know who he was, so that we could get our ride to where we would be laying our heads to rest from our long overseas flight.

There was much commotion and a multitude of people standing on the other side of the glass plate doors and windows. Eventually I decided that I needed to contact our hosts. Perhaps they had not received the message of our arrival. Sure enough, I was able to reach our host, and he was soon on his way to get us.

We were to spend the night on the compound of the Nigerian Bible Society, resting for the next part of our journey.

The next morning we were brought word that we would be having breakfast nearby with the gentleman himself, head of the Nigerian Bible Society. He greeted us and welcomed us into his lovely home to have breakfast with him.

Yes, he was most definitely a faithful tea drinker as we were. We sat at his beautiful dining table enjoying our breakfast and talking about many of his great adventures, and we soon learned that one of his dearest friends, Ruth Ward Heflin, was one of our dearest friends. He, too, had been to her home on Mount Zion and had dined under her pergola, many times drinking tea and eating the most delectable meals with other dignitaries from around the world. That one fact, that he was a friend of our dear friend, joined us together as we drank tea and ate with this great man of God.

After breakfast, he drove us through the streets of Lagos, and the most amazing sights were presented to us—some beautiful and some heart-wrenching. He then brought us to a marketplace as he picked up some things he needed.

As time for our flight to Freetown was fast approaching, we were then taken to the airport once again to head for our appointed destination. I must say that I have had invitations to return to Nigeria and to speak in meetings. I have not yet accepted those invites, but feel that before my days come to an end, I will once again visit Lagos, Nigeria and enjoy drinking many more cups of "Nigerian Tea."

Freetown, Sierra Leon and Royal Albert's Old Country Rose

And Many Cups of "Old Country Rose Tea"

Sierra Leone was colonized in 1787 by freed slaves arriving from England; other groups followed from Nova Scotia (1792) and Jamaica (1800). They were sponsored and governed by the private Sierra Leone Company until 1808, when Britain made Sierra Leone a crown colony. Freetown was so named because of the freed slaves that came there from Britain and North America and the "captives" taken off of slave ships on the Atlantic after Britain passed the 1807 Abolition of the Slave Trade. Sierra Leone remained under British rule until April 27, 1961.

We had no idea where or with whom we would be staying once we reached our destination. Our host, Desmond Thomas, was waiting for us at the airport. Because the airport was on the other side of the Sierra Leone River, we had to take a very much African ferry to get into Freetown.

In time, we arrived at a very large, several-story home that was gated and with armed guards, and we soon found ourselves meeting and staying in the most amazing and wonderful place.

We were the guests of Dr. Walter Sydney Marcus-Jones a former Chief Justice of the Supreme Court of Sierra Leon, and I would have the honor of becoming friends with his endearing, loving and elegant wife, Anne Marcus-Jones.

Our living area, during our stay in Freetown, would be in their home on the third floor, which was their living, dining, kitchen and sleeping area. Each of these rooms had French glass doors with curtains that opened to their large veranda.

Since we were on the third floor of their home, when we sat on the veranda to eat, visit with each other or have tea (which was several times a day), we were sitting up in the tops of banana trees, mango and papaya trees, coconut and great palm trees. And when we peered through the lush branches of those very large-leafed fruit-bearing trees, we could see the Atlantic Ocean, not all that far from their home. What a beautiful sight!

The Sierra Leonean Civil War

In 1991, the beautiful and peaceful, West African country of Sierra Leone was suddenly plunged into a brutal civil war that lasted for eleven long years and devastated the country and its people. This civil war was one of the bloodiest in African history, resulting in more than fifty thousand people dead and half a million displaced in a nation of only four million inhabitants.

The conflict was particularly violent and long because both sides were often funded by the infamous "blood diamonds" mined with slave labor.

Another brutal aspect of the war was the use of child soldiers and the practice of maiming opponents by hacking off their hands, arms or legs, leaving vast numbers of people permanently damaged.

My first encounter with my new-found friend, Anne, was amazing, for she was a very gracious and charm-filled lady, and she was inviting me to sit on the third-floor veranda as she brought out her prized Royal Albert's Country Rose Tea Set for us to have a pot of tea.

I was so amazed to see one of the most famous and most beloved tea sets around the world being set before me in a country that had been war-torn just a few short years before our visit. During our times of sharing our many cups of tea together, she would tell me how she and her husband, a supreme court judge in Sierra Leon, had to leave their home behind in Freetown and flee for their lives. It was the bloodiest war in African history. The civil war lasted for eleven years and left a massive path of destruction and devastation. A multitude of their people were slaughtered and all because of the diamond mines.

Once Anne and her husband had left the country, the rebels took over their home and ripped out everything that could be taken from it. While we were staying there, besides having a massive steel wall around their home and grounds, there were also armed guards posted at a guard shack to protect the Marcus-Jones family and their guests.

When they were finally able to return to their beloved home and city, there was nothing but devastation as far as their eyes could see. Their home was stripped of everything down to its concrete structure. Our dear brother, Mr. Marcus-Jones not only continued as a justice on the Supreme Court, but he also worked with the United Nations in the restoration of his beloved city and country.

I was in Freetown to speak in a wonderful women's conference. I also spoke in regular church services and at a church in another location.

During our stay, I was given many beautiful African garments that I cherished. They would wrap a scarf around my head and fixed it so that I eventually began to look like one of them and dance like one of them.

No women were allowed to minister with their heads uncovered. There were many miracles, signs, wonders and salvations. And, I came to have a very deep love for the people of Africa in Freetown and all of Sierra Leon but also in Ghana and Nigeria!

Anne Marcus-Jones became a very close and loving friend over the years. While I was in her home as her guest, she lavished us with bed linens soaked in the fragrance of lavender, and we shared in drinking many, many cups of "Old Rose Tea."

When my friend would go to California to visit her children, she called me several times while she was there. During our last phone call, she told me that the next year, when she would return to California, I would be there with her, because I was now part of the family. A few months after that we received a phone call from our dear fellow minister, Desmond Thomas. He wanted to let us know that my elegant and loving friend, a great woman of God from a war-torn country in Africa, who had served me tea in Royal Albert's Old Country Rose, had passed away. My heart was broken, and yet I rejoiced, for Anne was now on streets of gold.

For those who were not my people, have become my people!

— Romans 9:25

The time had now come for us to return home to the states. We would have one more stop on the way. But first we had to get back across the river to the airport. We had taken a ferry into town. This time, the ferry was out of service, so the only way to get to the airport was by helicopter. It was to be my very first helicopter ride.

But this would not be like anything you might have experienced yourself, wherever you might live. We would each be given a seat, but there was no space for our luggage, including our large check-on bags and our carry-on bags that we would have taken on board our flights to get to our destination. Every piece of our luggage, no matter how big or heavy it was, had to be placed on our laps. No one else could help me because they also had the same dilemma.

We truly did not think we were going to make it across the river to get to the airport. The helicopter vibrated so powerfully, and the vibration never stopped. The whole helicopter shook violently, trying to get into the air and then never stopped shaking until we finally reached our destination. I am so thankful for a faithful God who protects us and keeps us!

Haarlem, Netherlands
And a cup of "Corrie ten Boom Tea"

If you look at the world,. you'll be distressed. If you look within, you'll be depressed. But if you look at Christ, you'll be at rest!

— Corrie ten Boom —

Another layover would take us back to the Netherlands, the land of tea, chocolate, Delft china, tulips, daffodils and explosions of color.

This time we would find ourselves at Corrie Ten Boom's home, the site of the well-known book, The Hiding Place, located above Casper's Watch Shop.

Corrie ten Boom was a Dutch Christian who trained to be a watchmaker and, in 1922, became the first woman licensed as a watchmaker in Holland. She worked with her father, Casper ten Boom, in his Haarlem shop. During the next ten years, besides working as a watchmaker, she established a youth club for teenage girls, which provided religious instruction, as well as classes in the performing arts, sewing and handicrafts.

Corrie and her sister Betsie helped to hide many Jewish people from the Nazis during the Holocaust, thus her book, The Hiding Place. In time, Corrie and Betsie were captured and put into a concentration camp called Ravensbruck. While in the concentration camp, she shared the hope that she had in Jesus Christ with her fellow prisoners. Betsy died in Ravensbruck twelve days before Corrie was released without a reason.

With Jesus, even in our darkest moments, the best remains and the very best is yet to be!

– Corrie ten Boom -

Corrie ten Boom's home was a very amazing place to visit. After the tour, we were led to a beautiful room with lovely furniture and tea sets. There we were served a warm cup of tea in a beautiful china tea set pattern that Corrie ten Boom loved. So it was that in remembrance to a life well spent for the Kingdom of God, we drank a cup of "Corrie ten Boom Tea."

In Closing, There are Many Other Countries
Many Cups of "Jamaican Tea"

As we come to the close of this book, I must say that there will have to be another book of *A Southern Lady's Tea Adventures*! This book has run out of space, and there are many other countries that I have not shared with you as yet. But I will highlight them here briefly, just to whet your appetite.

I mentioned earlier in the book that my dear companion I traveled with to Israel would, two days after the closing of our trip, be traveling with me once again, this time to Jamaica. There had been other trips for me to Jamaica for the same hostess—Kim Puffpaff. On this trip, as we usually did, we flew into Kingston. There were two other ladies traveling with me. When we were greeted at the airport by my hostess, we were escorted by car to an undisclosed location. When we finally reached our destination, we found ourselves on the northern coast of Jamaica at a most beautiful resort, reserved just for our group. We had been brought to Ocho Rios, and our resort was right on the Caribbean Sea. This is where I would minister. Here, of course, we shared our time with these amazing women and for morning breakfast, lunch, an afternoon pick-me-up and again in the evening, we were brought, as you can already imagine, many wonderful cups of "Jamaican Tea."

A Trip to Rome, Aversa, and Naples, Italy
With many cups of "Aversa Afternoon Tea"

When in Rome, do as the Romans do!

I loved Rome and who would not? We were in Rome for just a couple of days because we were on a mission to do crusades in Naples, or as the Italian's would say, *Napoli.*

We visited the Vatican and Saint Peter's Square, the Sistine Chapel, which was built in 1479 and houses the most famous painted interior with the most famous of all, the ceilings painted by Michelangelo from 1508 to 1512. Everything was absolutely breathtaking to behold.

We also visited the Coliseum where 3000 Christians were martyred. It is a historical and magnificent structure that was filled with extreme brutality. Christian's were slaughtered there over a 40-year period.

We visited the Royal Palace of Caserta, which was most amazing and beautiful. It would take another book to describe everything our eyes beheld there, but I will say one of the things I absolutely loved in the palace was a gift from Marie Antoinette to the King of Naples. It was a gilded birdcage with a little bird automaton sitting on a swing. When a lever was moved, the little bird automaton would move and sing and chirp.

This palace was the residence constructed by the House of Bourbon-Two Sicilies brothers as their place of dwelling while they were the Kings of Naples. It was the largest palace built in Europe in the 18th century. They had first built a fort on the Mediterranean Sea, which we also visited. The Fort was their home at first, but they decided to build a palace as their residence much further inland. They left the fort operational, with soldiers as a defense against their enemies to protect them and their inland palace.

Our hotel in Rome was a very quaint and lovely hotel, which I loved. We would have our breakfasts in the hotel in their breakfast room that had floor-to-ceiling pink drapes and simple wrought-iron tables with white table cloths. It was not an elaborate hotel, rather obscure, but as I said previously, very quaint and lovely. Our Italian breakfast with our cups of tea was such a delightfully enjoyable time and was always served with chocolate.

One of the things that I fell in love with at this hotel in Rome was what I considered a work of art—a black wrought-iron elevator. It was black wrought-iron on all four sides, and you could see right through it to the other side and you could see from the top floor all the way down to the bottom. While in Rome, I continued to drink my many cups of tea.

It was not until we reached our destination, Aversa, Italy, the place where we would be lodging during the crusade meetings that I began to "do as the Romans do" and drink the real Italian cappuccino every day. Others continued their loyalty to cups of black tea. Even though it may seem like I jumped ship, so to speak, by drinking Italian cappuccino, I still continued every day to have my cups of a delicious black Italian tea, "Aversa Afternoon Tea."

Aversa is an ancient city steeped in history. There was a wonderful place there called the "Pink House," where I learned to love, not only freshly-made cappuccino, but also the wonderful Italian pastry called cornettos, meaning "little horns." Cornettos are Italian croissants, but they are filled with delicious homemade fillings. My favorite flavor was chocolate. I later made chocolate cornettos for my tea parties back home, and everyone loved them. I will have the very quick and easy recipe in my next book, *A Southern Lady's Teas*.

We were then on to the crusades, which were held outside of Naples. We were in these crusades to be of help to Jeremy LaBorde. I was one of the speakers. There were many great miracles with many lives touched for the Kingdom of God. At the end of the services, we would all gather at a wonderful outdoor restaurant under the stars. The moon was so big, and it seemed, night after night, to set itself right over our dining area under the heavens.

Quito, Ecuador

And Many Cups of "Ecuadorian Yerba Mate"

We were invited to Ecuador to participate in the 80th birthday celebration of Pastor Zenon Rivera. One of our companions had lived in Ecuador for 8 years, and many of those years were spent working closely with Pastor Zenon, in establishing churches, training ministers, conducting campmeetings and crusades, and even overseeing a home for children of the street.

It was my first time in Quito, and for me, it was a delight, from the lovely Spanish architecture, the mysterious Andes mountains and the wonderful people, their colorful dress and their delicious foods. I particularly enjoyed seeing the indigenous Quichua Indian people in their native costumes, hearing their lovely music and seeing their beautiful dances. The ox roast was also something to behold and enjoy.

The capital city, Quito, situated at nearly 10,000 feet of altitude, is breathtakingly beautiful and even higher mountains surround it. When the clouds occasionally parted and we caught a glimpse of the snowcapped volcanoes Ecuador is famous for, it was truly awe-inspiring. It was our privilege to stay and speak in the two-thousand seat coliseum that is now home to the ministry Pastor Zenon birthed so many years ago.

One of the highlights of the trip was when the current pastor of the church, Ramiro Padilla, took us to eat at a restaurant situated near the equator. I could never have imagined it. We were taken to many beautiful places to eat and to have tea, but this day, after going to the equator, we were taken to a very lovely place to dine. We sat next to a large window, and as I looked out of the window, we were sitting on the edge of a dormant volcano. We were encouraged to look a little further, and inside the crater there were homes and farmland, with different plots filled with an abundance of crops.

As we sat there eating, we were at such a high altitude that we were in the clouds, and white fluffy clouds moved in between the upper edges of the volcano and slowly drifted over the crater, covering our view of the crops, the farmers and their homes.

Another beautiful place that we stopped to get some afternoon tea was on the world famous Calle La Ronda, also known as the Juan de Dios Morales Street, which is steeped in history. This beautiful street is a delight to the eyes, with wonderful shops filled with Panama hats, Quito's delectable chocolates, doors and windows decorated with geraniums, wrought iron and flags—all picture worthy. La Ronda is a street of antiquity and is said to be the oldest area of Quito. In 1531, during the Spanish Conquest, the conquistadors took Ecuador and began to establish Quito with its street of antiquity, Calle La Ronda. It was here that we stopped to have a cup of a very strong "Ecuadorian Green Tea, Yerba Mate."

Sydney, Australia

Warming Cups of "Twinings Australian Afternoon Tea" and "Roibos Tea"

I was invited to speak in a conference in the Dallas/Fort Worth area, and there I met a beautiful Nigerian lady who was living in Australia with her husband and children. She and her husband were pastoring a Nigerian Church in Sydney. I would soon receive an invitation to go to Sydney to speak in their church, but also to be the speaker in her very large annual women's conference. There would be many women (and men) there from Nigeria, but there would also be many Australian Nationals in the meetings.

After all the speaking was over, my hostess and her husband were gracious enough to take us sightseeing. We were taken to the famous Blue Mountains, one of the homes to the Indigenous Aboriginal peoples of Australia. They have lived there for more than 5,000 years in that habitat for the koala bears, kangaroos, dingoes and so much more.

Although it was the heat of summer when we left home, it was winter in Australia and quite cold while we were there. I loved the break from our summer heat.

We were happy to visit some beautiful gift shops when leaving the mountainous area. We stopped to get a bite to eat and were able to have a wonderful hot cup of that country's black tea, Twinings Australia Afternoon Tea. It was a hardy, delicious and warming cup of tea. We were also able to enjoy their rich Roibos Tea.

They then brought us to a wonderful large church service where a marvelous production was being performed. It was very cold as we sat outside to eat before the service. Here again, we enjoyed being offered a hot cup of tea to warm us. This time, I so appreciated a hearty cup of Earl Grey.

Our journey was not over yet. We next found ourselves in the heart of Sydney and were able to experience the massive Light Show. It was like nothing we had ever seen or experienced before—truly magnificent. Words cannot express the dimensions and different forms that were displayed and filled the Harbor of Sydney. It would take another book just to give you a glimpse into what our eyes beheld. People by the millions travel to Sydney every year to see this marvelous light experience that covers every inch of the harbor's buildings and bridges. We were left in awe!

It was interesting to me to find that many of the older homes in this area of Australia, mostly in Sydney and Melbourne, had a very strong Victorian style, due to the influence of Queen Victoria and the beautiful Victorian Age. This was true, not only in the architecture of the homes, but also in public buildings and tearooms etc. These tearooms were very beautiful and elegant, with chandeliers, satin and plush velvet seating and pillows and the most delicious displays of food for afternoon tea, even known as high tea in some of their finest tearooms!

And now I would like to introduce you to my Featured Guests.

The next 52 pages will fill your eyes with beauty and delight. Since this Southern Lady's tea book had an international flavor to it, I only thought it appropriate to bring a little international flavor through my guests and their recipes. I know you will enjoy reading their incredible bios. Their recipes are amazing, yet easy enough to incorporate them into your own special tea parties, afternoon teas or a special tea for two. The photos you will see accompanying each guest's recipes are their own photography, and I find they are beautiful and show off their recipes to perfection. Each are well seasoned cooks, tea enthusiasts, "lovers of everything tea," and "lovers of everything beautiful!"

We had two more guest that we wanted to feature, but they will be in in the third book of A Southern Lady's tea series, A Southern Lady's Teas.

Featured Guests

Paul Ryan T. Co
Metro Manila, Philippines

Melanie Bazell
San Diego, California

Tina Strangis
Melbourne, Australia

Kitty Penrod
Frisco, Texas

Paul Ryan T. Co

The Co Family of the Philippines are avid tea consumers with a rich history of tea heritage. The family's eldest son, Paul Ryan T. Co is a world traveler, an entrepreneur, an antique collector and a tea enthusiast who continues to pursue his family's inherent passion for tea. He is also a part-time caterer and baker based in Metro Manila, capital city of the beautiful islands of the Philippines, a country in the East Indies along the Western Pacific coast of South-East Asia.

Paul has lived and traveled around different countries across Asia, North America and Europe, where he diligently researched and recorded different tea-related customs from different cultures and regions. During his residency and travels abroad, he visited the Oolong tea plantations in the Alishan Mountain range township of Taiwan, to observe the processing and to sample the tea produced from plantations located in mountainous altitudes of up to 1,600 meters. He has visited tea plantations from the Westlake region of Hangzhou to observe the processing and grading of the famed Longjing (Dragon well) green teas, where the highest grade of such teas sell for more than the price of gold by the gram and are still being produced from leaves harvested from the original eighteen tea bushes granted Imperial status during the Qing Dynasty that are now over 400 years old.

Paul's family continues to enjoy strong ties with relatives from their native ancestral village in Fujian, procuring many rare teas exclusively found in that region's heritage tea plantations. He has had the pleasure of partaking in afternoon teas hosted and held in many historic locations, such as London, Paris and Vancouver— Kensington Palace, the Pail Court at the Ritz, Harrods Tea Rooms, the Savoy, the Empress and Brown's.

Paul continues to advocate and promote the preservation of tea-related customs, traditions and ceremonies from all cultures by incorporating ancient tea-time practices from all over the world. His estate and garden-based catering, aptly named the "Vintage Rolling Pin," specializes in catered afternoon teas and historically-themed tea party events. He has hosted tea parties in the family's three quarters of an acre gardens, which consists of the family's numerous gardens, patios, verandas, courtyards and orchards, where they harvest fruits from nearly century-old fruit trees planted by his grandparents, to be used in his afternoon tea recipes. As has been practiced for generations by his family, visitors and guests alike have been enjoying his hosted afternoon teas, using pieces from the family's vast collection of silver, china, Victorian and Edwardian furniture and fine monogrammed linen surrounded by perfumed tropical gardens with views of ponds, flora and fauna. His afternoon and high tea menus include re-creations of traditional international heritage dishes, desserts and pastries, using vintage recipes from different cultures, which are then presented and served in period authentic settings.

Paul's love and passion for tea can be traced back to his heritage. He and his family are descendants of an ancient tea-farming clan from a village in the Southern Fujian Province of China that farmed and produced not only tea but also lychees and tangerine-hued sweet potatoes. His ancestors trace their lineage back to the Tang Dynasty, when an Imperial Tang Dynasty general and his troops were stationed in the region and established the village with their families to farm its fertile earth. The region's tea plantations in his ancestral farming village are renowned for developing the Tieguanyin (Iron Goddess Tea) a variety of oolong tea still being processed in the region using ancient methods to produce the tea so enjoyed around the world until today.

Ensaymada

Perhaps the most common and well-loved sweet pastry delicacy in the Philippines, the ensaymada is a light, buttery brioche bun topped with grated cheese, butter and sugar and is commonly enjoyed during the afternoons. The pastry bun was adapted from an early recipe of the Mallorcan ensaïmada introduced to the islands by 16th century Spanish colonists. It is the Philippine equivalent, in terms of consumption and significance, to the American biscuit and the British scone and is always present in the afternoon snack table to accompany coffee, hot chocolate or tea.

Ingredients for the brioche bun:
- ½ cup butter
- 1 cup evaporated milk
- 5 Tablespoons sugar
- ½ Teaspoon salt
- 2 eggs
- 1 Tablespoon active dry yeast
- 3 ½ cup plain flour or bread flour

Ingredient for the toppings:
- 1 cup of mild Cheddar or American cheese grated
- 1/2 cup of hard Edam or Parmesan cheese grated
- ½ cup castor sugar
- ¼ cup softened butter

Method:
1. In a large pot, melt the butter over low heat then add the milk & sugar. Stir until sugar is melted. Remove from heat and let stand for 2 minutes until just warm but not hot.
2. Add the salt, yeast and the eggs then mix well in the warm pot.
3. Slowly add the sifted flour while mixing well with a wooden spoon to from a sticky dough. Continue mixing for 5 minutes.
4. Cover the pot and let the dough proof in the pot for 1 hour.
5. Remove risen dough and knead on a lightly floured surface or in an electric stand mixer using the dough hook attachment for 15 to 20 minutes, until dough is elastic.
6. Divide dough into 16 equal portions.
7. Form each portion into a 10" log and coil tightly.
8. Individually place each coiled bun dough into buttered large muffin tins or small 3" to 4" cake tins.
9. Cover in a lightly damped cloth or kitchen towel in a warm area to proof for another hour.
10. Bake in a 350°F preheated oven for 18 to 20 minutes
11. Let cool till just warm and brush tops with melted butter before dunking in sugar and sprinkle with a generous mixture of American with Edam or Parmesan Cheese.

Empanada

Philippine empanadas are traditional meat-stuffed crescent-shaped turnover pastry pies introduced to the Philippines by Galician friars from Spain during the early 1600s. They have been adapted locally, using available native Philippine ingredients and spices and have evolved throughout the centuries to what is now a favorite afternoon snack-time treat renowned for their sweet and savory fillings, as well as their light and flaky pastry crusts.

Ingredients for the Filling:

- 1 pound pork, minced or finely diced in the food processor
- 1 medium potato, finely diced
- 1 medium carrot, finely diced
- 2 hard-boiled eggs, chopped
- 1 medium-sized red onion, diced
- 2 minced garlic cloves
- ¼ cup raisins
- 1 teaspoon salt
- ¼ teaspoon ground pepper
- 1 tablespoon Worcestershire Sauce
- 1 tablespoon sugar
- ½ cup water or stock

Ingredients for the dough:
- 3¼ cups all-purpose flour
- 1/2 teaspoon salt
- 1 cup unsalted butter, cut into small cubes
- 1 egg
- 10 tablespoons milk

Ingredients for the egg wash:
whites of 1 egg
2 tablespoons milk

Method:
1. In a covered skillet or saucepan, sauté garlic and onions in oil until fragrant but not brown. Add in the pork and cook on high until halfway through.
2. Add raisins, Worcestershire Sauce and water or stock. Cover the skillet. Adjust the heat to medium. Cook for 10 to 12 minutes.
3. Add the rest of the ingredients. Stir, cover and cook on low for 8 to 10 minutes until vegetables are tender and stock significantly reduced. Remove from heat and set aside to cool.

For easy homemade dough:
* Alternatively, you can use pre-made grocery biscuit or puff pastry dough. Separate 1 tube of dough into 12 to 14 portions. Do not form into a ball. Directly press or roll each dough portion to form 4-inch round disks.
1. Put flour in a food processor and add salt. Pulse until both ingredients are well blended.
2. Add butter into the food processor, 1 cube at a time, while continuing to pulse until all the butter has been added and has blended well with the flour mixture, forming a crumble.
3. Add the egg and gradually add the milk, 2 to 3 tablespoons at a time, while pulsing. Continue to process the mixture until all the ingredients are well blended into a clay-like ball of dough.
4) Transfer the dough onto a lightly-floured flat surface. With lightly-floured hands, shape the dough into a large ball. With a dough cutter, cut the ball in half and, using a lightly-floured rolling pin, roll each dough into a thick 1" disk. Chill the dough for at least 20 minutes.
5. After 20 minutes, remove the dough from the fridge and roll each piece of dough on a flat surface using a rolling pin until it is around .10" thick.
6. Cut dough into circular disks using a 4" cookie cutter.

Assembling the Pork Empanada:
1. Place 1 to 2 tablespoons of the pork filling in the center of the circular dough. Secure it by folding both sides of the dough inward toward each other. Use your thumb and index finger to pinch the sides so they will cling to each other. Crimp edges by pressing the tines of a fork on the pinched edges of the empanada.
2. Arrange the empanadas on a baking tray lined with parchment paper. Bake for 15 minutes in an oven, pre-heated to 350° F, then remove from the oven.
3. Prepare the egg wash by combining egg white and milk in a bowl. Beat the mixture until blended. Brush the egg wash all over the top of the empanadas.
4. Put the pork empanadas back into the oven. Continue to bake for 10 to 15 minutes or until they turn medium brown.

Brazo De Mercedes

A traditional Philippine dessert, Brazo de Mercedes is a meringue-based jelly roll from the Spanish colonial period of the Philippines, dating back to the 17th century. Its Spanish name literally translates to the "Arm of our Lady of Mercy." Food historians believe that the origins of this lighter-than-air roll cake was developed some 300 years ago from a Spanish Granadian roll cake recipe brought over to the islands by Spanish conquistadors, which was then adapted locally and adjusted to re-purpose the excess eggs left over from the mortar and plaster finishing of a church.

Ingredients:

10 large eggs at room temperature with the yolks and whites separated
½ teaspoon cream of tartar
1 teaspoon vanilla extract
¾ cup granulated sugar
¼ cup powdered sugar
zest of 1 lemon
14 ounces condensed milk

Method:

1. Line a cookie sheet or jelly pan with parchment and lightly grease the parchment.
2. In a stand mixer or a bowl, using an electric mixer, beat the egg whites until foamy.
3. Add cream of tartar while continuously beating until soft peaks form.
4. Gradually add the sugar in 4 stages, while increasing the speed with every addition until stiff peaks form.
5. Evenly distribute the meringue mixture onto the prepared and parchment-lined pan. Spread evenly using a spatula. Decorate with an icing comb run along the length.
6. Bake the meringue in an oven pre-heated to 350° F for 20 to 22 minutes until the color of the meringue turns light to medium brown.
7. While the meringue is in the oven, make the custard filling by combining the egg yolks, zest and condensed milk in a small saucepan.
8. Cook over medium heat, while continuously stirring until the texture becomes thick like soft custard.
9. Add the vanilla extract to the custard. Turn off the heat and mix thoroughly. Set aside.
10. Remove the meringue from the oven and let it cool for a few minutes.
11. To unmold the meringue, dust the top of the meringue with powdered sugar. Then place a sheet of waxed paper over it, enough to cover meringue. Place a spare baking pan or a tray bottom down on to the meringue and flip the meringue. The top of the meringue sheet is now sitting on the waxed paper on top of the spare tray. Gently unmold from the baking pan and peel off the parchment. The inside of the meringue sheet cake is now facing up.
12. Evenly spread the custard filling on the inside of the meringue sheet cake with a spatula.
13. Roll the meringue along the longer length so that the custard filling is now inside the jelly roll.
14. Secure the jelly roll in the waxed paper and let the roll set in the refrigerator overnight.
15. Dust with powdered sugar and garnish with lemon zest just before serving.

Mango Cake

The tropical and subtropical climate across the Philippines makes it ideal to grow large and sweet mangoes, which are harvested twice a year. The Philippines is known for its plump, juicy and sweet golden mangoes. The fruit can be found in many local recipes across the islands. This recipe incorporates sweet mangoes into a light chiffon-based layered cake, frosted in light and easy Chantilly-style cream icing. A nod to the light fruit-topped cakes over génoise sponge ever popular in Asia and in many Asian bakeries, the incorporation of mangoes and light icing makes this a guilt free delicious treat ideal for tea time.

Ingredients for the egg batter:
  1 cup Cake flour
  ¼ cup sugar
  1 ½ Teaspoon baking powder
  ¼ Teaspoon salt
  4 egg yolks
  ¼ cup canola oil or vegetable oil
  1/3 cup milk
  ¼ cup puree of mango or puree of 1 small mango
  1 Teaspoon vanilla extract
  1 Teaspoon mango extract

Ingredient for the meringue:
  4 egg whites
  ½ cup white sugar
  ½ Teaspoon cream of tartar

Ingredients for the toppings and filling:
  2 cups sweet mango, diced
  2 Tablespoon corn flour
  ¼ cup sugar
  ½ cup mango puree
  ¼ cup cold water

Ingredients for the frosting:
  2 cups whipping cream (refrigerated overnight)
  1/2 cup powder sugar
  1 Teaspoon vanilla extract
  2 Teaspoon gelatin powder (clear and unflavored)

Method:
For the mango filling, which you can make a day in advance.

1. In a saucepan, gently heat the mango puree on low and add sugar, while continuously stirring until the sugar is completely melted.
2. Add the corn flour that has been dissolved in cold water. Turn up heat to medium and stir continuously for 1 to 2 minutes until the sauce starts to thicken but is not bubbling.

3. Add the mango cubes and cover 3 minutes over medium heat.
4. Remove cover and gently stir for 2 minutes until the sauce has completely thickened and reduced, forming a mango compote. Remove from heat to cool completely.

For the Cake:
1. In an electric stand mixer or a bowl, using a hand mixer, beat the yellows of 4 eggs with the sugar on high until it turns pale yellow. Add in oil, extracts and puree, while continually mixing until well combined.
2. In a bowl, sift to combine the dry ingredients: flour, baking powder and salt. Mix until well blended.
3. Slowly add the dry ingredients to the egg mixture in alternate with the milk until just combined where you see no dry flour left. * Do not over mix. Set aside.
4. Beat egg whites using a hand mixer on medium-low speed until foamy. Add cream of tartar while slowly adding the sugar in 4 steps as you increase speed until stiff peaks form.
5. Gently fold meringue into the base batter just until blended. *Do not over mix.
6. Gently divide the cake batter into the pan/s lined with parchment paper on the bottom. * Do not grease the sides of the pan/s.
7. Bake in oven pre-heated to 325° F for 45 minutes.
8. Turn the pan/s upside down into the cooling rack and let them cool completely inverted.
9. To un-mold cake after cooling, run an offset spatula or knife around the inner pan blade parallel to wall of pan to separate the cake from the pan. Cake should fall off the pan easily after you flip it. Peel parchment and level the cakes.

* Alternatively, you may also use ready-boxed cake mixes available from your local grocery stores. Choose a vanilla or a white cake chiffon box cake mix. Replace water or milk in the boxed cake mix instructions with mango juice, and add 1 teaspoon of mango extract. Follow the rest of the boxed cake instructions.

For the Chantilly-Style Whipped Cream Frosting
1. Chill mixing bowl and beaters for 15-30 minutes in the fridge or freezer.
2. Combine gelatin powder and warm water. Mix until it dissolves. Then cool slightly.
3. Pour the whip into the chilled bowl and, using an electric hand blender, beat until soft peaks form on medium speed.
4. Add vanilla extract and sugar.
5. Increase speed to medium high and add dissolved gelatin.
6. Whip until stiff peaks form.

Assembling the cake:
1. Level and divide the cakes into 3 sheets.
2. Spread mango compote on the first layer evenly.
3. Spread whipped cream frosting evenly on the other half.
4. Place it frosting-side-down on the first layer.
5. Repeat steps for the remaining layers.
6. Cover the cake with whipped cream frosting.
7. Pipe extra whipped cream on the top circumference edge of the cake to serve as a wall to hold in the toppings. You may garnish the top of the cake with fresh sliced mangoes or with the remainder of the mango compote.
* Let the assembled cake set in the refrigerator overnight or for at least 2 hours before serving.

Smoked Fish Canape

As an archipelagic country composed of more than 7,600 islands in the Western Pacific Ocean, the Philippines has a wide and abundant access to fish and shellfish. Seafood is a staple in Philippine cuisine and is present in many native recipes throughout the islands. This recipe incorporates smoked seafood and shellfish (locally known as "Tinapa") into an elegant canapé perfect for hors d'oeuvres and light savory afternoon treats.

Ingredients:

1 small can smoked fish around 100grams or 5oz. Any kind such as smoked salmon or trout.
8oz cream cheese
3 Tablespoons finely chopped green onions
3 Tablespoons mayonnaise
1 Teaspoon garlic powder
1 Teaspoon paprika
1 Teaspoon ground pepper
3 Tablespoons chopped dill

Method:

1. Drain the canned smoked fish. Place in paper towel to absorb as much liquid as possible.
2. Manually flake the drained fish by raking down with a fork until well separated.
3. In mixing bowl, blend cream cheese and mayonnaise until creamy.
4. Add all other ingredients and mix well.
5. Spread or pipe on toast, crackers or crostini.
6. Garnish with dill, cooked shrimp, smoked baby oysters or caviar.

Melanie Bazell

Malanie's love affair with tea and tea-ware began when she was a young girl working in a family teashop. Later in life, her passion for tea grow when she married a man who was both British and a tea enthusiast.

Her family owned a store called Violettes of London. They sold tea, curds, jams and Beatrix Potter teapots. Her aunt and cousin provided afternoon tea catering for special clients. Melanie worked mostly nights and weekends.

It was a beautiful store that smelled wonderfully of roses and lavenders, potpourris of every fragrance, Crabtree and Evelyn soaps, floral umbrellas, and Victorian pewter hairbrushes.

During the holiday season the whole family worked together, which made it all the more special. The store was decorated with Victorian Santas and cherubs and smelled of hot spiced apple cider.

She wrote, "What I wouldn't give to travel back in time and relive those days with my family, many of whom have passed away. I truly believe those beautiful early life experiences shaped my love of afternoon tea. I love hosting afternoon tea for a friend or more and creating a special environment where we can spend the afternoon together sharing our time and opening our hearts.

"I hope you will enjoy the vegan/plant-based versions of my favorite afternoon tea recipes! Please know that these recipes are for everyone. The flavor is in no way compromised. They are delectably delicious, rich in flavor, and shared with kindness and love."

Cherry Chocolate Mousse

COURSE: Desserts
 2 servings

INGREDIENTS
 * 1 avocado, ripe
 * 2 tablespoons raw cacao powder or cocoa
   powder
 * 2 to 3 tablespoons maple syrup
 * 1/2 teaspoon vanilla
 * pinch salt
 * 2 tablespoons water or more as needed to
   blend
 * 1/2 cup frozen cherries

INSTRUCTIONS
 * Add all above ingredients into a mini-
   processor or blender and blend until
   smooth.
 * Can be eaten immediately. (Tastes even
   better when refrigerated over night!)
 * Refrigerate and eat within 72 hours.

Feel free to add any frozen fruit (raspberries,
  cherries, blueberries are all delicious!) You
  can also use nuts. I highly recommend
  adding frozen cherries!

English Lavender Scones

* 2 cups all-purpose flour
* 1 tbsp baking powder
* 1/4 cup sugar
* Vegan butter 1/3 cup
* Aqua Faba 1/3 cup
* Almond milk 3 tbs
* ½ tsp salt
* 1 tbs vanilla extract
* 1/3 cup dry fruit of choice
* 1/4 lavender (food grade)

Course: Afternoon Tea, High Tea, Snack Cuisine:
British, English,

Vegan Prep Time: 30 minutes
Cook Time: 15-20 minutes
Time: 45 minutes
Servings: 8
Calories: 290 cal

For the Scones

* Pre-heat oven to 350. C
* Pour flour into a bowl, then add the sugar.
* Rub the vegan butter into the mixture with your fingers until the mixture looks crumbly.
* If using dried fruit, add this to the mixture, and add the non-dairy milk.
* Add 1 tbs of vanilla extract
* Whisk the aquafaba using a whisk and a separate bowl for 1 to 2 minutes.
* Pour the whisked aquafaba into the dough mixture. Mix the mixture together with your hands. The dough should be soft but not too sticky. If the dough seems too dry, add more almond milk.(Do not over work the dough)
* Form the dough into a ball and cut the ball in half. Next, cut each half of the call into fourths. This technique helps you measure the size and portions of your scones.
* Use a cookie cutter to cut the dough. You may also us an clean food tin or glass. Make sure the dough is 2 inches thick. If too thin, the scones will not rise. Make sure the cutter goes all the way through the dough, and do not twist it, or the scones will be a strange shape.
* Put scones on a baking sheet and brush each with a little non-dairy milk.
* Put scones on the middle shelf of the oven. Bake for 15-20 minutes. They are done when they have risen and are a golden brown. Remove from oven and place on a cooling rack. Serve warm or cold with jam.

Lemon Tea Cake

Cake Ingredients

  Flower 1 1/2 cup
  Almond Flour 1/2 cup
  Butter 1/3 cup (or 5 tbs)
  Aqua Faba (garbanzo bean juice)1/3 cup
  Almond milk 1/2 cup
  Salt 1/2 teaspoon
  Baking soda 1 tbs
  Sugar 1/4 cup
  Baking powder 1 tbs
  Vanilla extract 1 tbs
  Dry fruit if chosen 1/3 cup
  Lemon juice 1 tbs
  Lemon zest 1 lemon.

Mix the following ingredients together in a separate bowl.

Icing Ingredients

  Lemon 2 tablesoons
  Powdered sugar 1 1/2 cups
  Butter 2 oz
  1/2 lemon zest

- Pre-heat oven to 350. C
- Pour flour into a bowl, then add the sugar.
- Rub the vegan butter into the mixture with your fingers until the mixture looks crumbly.
- If using dried fruit, add this to the mixture, and add the non-dairy milk.
- Add 1 tbs of vanilla extract
- Whisk the aquafaba using a whisk and a separate bowl for one to 2 minutes.
- Pour the whisked aquafaba into the dough mixture. Mix the mixture together with your hands. The dough should be soft but not too sticky. If the dough seems too dry, add more milk.(Do not over work the dough)
- Line the cake pan with a non stick oil or spray of your choice.
- Pour cake mixture into the cake pan.
- Bake for 20 to 30 minutes depending on your oven's temperature.
- Remove the cake and let the cake cool.
- Ice the cake.
- Add additional lemon zest for garnish.

Rose Petal Jam

Ingredients :

1. 1 ½ water
2. 2 ounces rose petals (approx. 2 cups gently packed. (Gathered 50 feet from roads and pesticide free) or 2/3 cup dried
3. 2 cups organic cane sugar
4. 3 tablespoons fresh lemon juice
5. 1 teaspoon fruit pectin

Directions:

1. Prepare the rose petals by washing and removing the petals.
2. Include water and roses in a saucepan. Bring to a low simmer for 10 minutes, without cover.
3. Add 1 ¾ cups of sugar into the simmering mixture . Stir gently to mix in the sugar.
4. Add lemon juice.
5. Simmer for 10 minutes on low heat.
6. In another bowl, combine the remaining ¼ cup sugar and pectin.
7. Stir the jam while adding the pectin/sugar mixture. Add this mixture by sprinkling in small amounts at a time to avoid clumping.
8. Simmer on low for 20 minutes.
9. The mixture becomes firm as it sets but remains slightly fluid.
10. This jam keeps fresh in the refrigerator for 2 months. You may also freeze or can to store for up to six months.

You can also make a rose petal jelly by straining out the rose petals and following the ingredients above.

Eggless Salad Sandwiches

Ingredients
- 1 block extra-firm tofu, drained & pressed
- 1/3 cup vegan mayo
- 1/4 cup finely chopped celery
- 1/4 cup finely chopped dill pickles
- 1/4 cup finely chopped onions
- 2 tablespoons mustard
- 2 tablespoons fresh dill (or 2 teaspoons dry)
- 1/2 teaspoon black salt (kala namak)
- 1/4 teaspoon black pepper
- 1/8 teaspoon smoked paprika
- 1/8 teaspoon turmeric

Directions
1. Chop the tofu into small pieces and transfer to a large bowl.
2. Add the remaining ingredients and stir well.
3. Cover and refrigerate for at least 30 minutes before eating.
4. Cut bread into small sizes. You can prepare three finger sandwiches per 2 slices of bread. Spread ingredients inside of the bread.

Tina Strangis

Tina Strangis, who lives in Melbourne, Australia, is married with two children. She has enjoyed baking from a young age. She worked as a café manager for quite a few years before opening her own café in partnership with her sister. She is now retired.

When she and her husband are not cruising on the high seas, she can be found either in her kitchen baking or pottering in the garden.

Monte Carlo Biscuits/Cookies

These biscuits are an old-fashioned Aussie favorite, with a filling of jam and vanilla cream. The recipe makes 25 biscuits/cookies.

- 3/4 cup butter, softened
- 1/2 cup brown sugar
- 2 cups all-purpose flour
- 1 egg
- 1/2 teaspoon baking powder
- 1/2 teaspoon baking soda
- 1 teaspoon vanilla extract
- 1 Tablespoon golden syrup or honey
- 2/3 cup coconut

- 3 Tablespoons butter, softened
- 1/2 teaspoon vanilla extract
- 3/4 cup icing sugar, sifted
- 2 teaspoons milk
- 1/3 cup raspberry jam

Preheat oven to 350F . Line two trays with baking paper.

Place softened butter and sugar in a bowl and beat with an electric mixer until light and fluffy.

Add egg, vanilla extract and golden syrup and beat well.

Add sifted dry ingredients and coconut and beat well.

Roll teaspoonfuls of mixture into balls, Place on lined oven trays. Flatten slightly and use a fork to make a criss-cross pattern.

Bake for 10 to 15 minutes or until a light golden brown. Remove from oven. Cool on a wire rack

Lamingtons

Lamingtons is an Australian classic, a soft buttery sponge cake coated with chocolate icing and coconut

- 1/2 cup butter, softened
- 1 cup white sugar
- 4 eggs
- 2 cups all-purpose flour
- 4 teaspoons baking powder
- 1 teaspoon vanilla extract
- pinch of salt
- 1/2 cup milk

Icing

- 3 cups icing sugar
- 3 Tablespoons cocoa powder
- 2 Tablespoons butter, softened
- 1/2 cup hot water
- 3 cups coconut

Preheat oven to 350 F. Line an 8"x12" rectangular cake pan with baking paper hanging over the two sides for easy removal.

Using electric beaters, cream the butter and sugar until light in color.

Add eggs one at a time, beating well after each addition.

Beat in vanilla extract.

Sift the flour, baking powder and salt over the butter mixture.

Add the milk and fold together until evenly combined.

Pour mixture into prepared pan, bake for 30-35 minutes or until a skewer inserted in the center comes out clean.

Turn out onto a wire rack to cool completely. Wrap tightly in plastic wrap and place in the freezer for a few hours or overnight.

Icing Mixture

Sift the icing sugar and cocoa powder into a bowl.

Add the butter, then pour in the hot water a little at a time. Stir until smooth and runny.

Place coconut in a shallow bowl.

Remove cake from freezer. While still frozen, cut into 20 pieces.

Using a bamboo skewer, dip the cake in the icing mixture. Then gently remove from skewer and toss lightly in the coconut to coat.

Place on a wire rack to set. Note: If icing mixture becomes too thick, add a little more hot water.

Passionfruit Yo-Yo Biscuits

Melt in the mouth buttery biscuits joined together with a delicious passionfruit buttercream. These are a true Aussie classic.

250 grams/ 1 cup butter, at room temperature
1/3 cup icing/ confectioners sugar
1 teaspoon vanilla extract
1 1/2 cups plain/ all purpose flour
1/2 cup custard powder.

Passionfruit Buttercream
65 grams/ 1/3 cup butter, at room temperature
1 cup icing/ confectioners sugar
2 Tablespoons passionfruit pulp

Preheat oven to 180c/ 350f Line two trays with baking paper.

Using electric beaters, cream the butter and icing sugar until pale and fluffy, add vanilla extract and beat well.

Sift flour and custard powder over butter mixture. Using a wooden spoon, stir to combine.

Roll rounded teaspoons of dough into balls. Place on prepared trays, and flatten with a lightly floured fork.

Bake for 15 minutes or until lightly golden underneath. Leave on trays for 5 minutes, then transfer to a wire rack to cool.

Passionfruit Buttercream
Using an electric mixer, beat butter, sifted icing sugar and passionfruit pulp in a small bowl until pale and fluffy. Spread or pipe the filling onto half the biscuits and sandwich with the other half.

3-Ingredient Lemonade Scones

Lemonade scones are fast and easy to make. They are light and fluffy and only require 3 ingredients.

- 3 1/2 cups self-rising flour. See note.
- 1 cup heavy cream
- 1 cup sprite/ 7-Up lemonade

Jam and Cream to serve.

Preheat oven to 390F . Line a tray with baking paper.

Sift flour into a large bowl.

Pour in lemonade and cream and mix to a soft dough.

Turn out onto a generously floured surface. Knead lightly for 1 minute. Then press dough into a 3/4 inch disc.

Using a 2-inch cutter, cut dough into rounds and place close together on the paper-lined baking tray. Gently knead scraps of dough together. Repeat pressing and cutting.

Lightly brush tops with a little extra cream and bake for 15-20 minutes or until a light golden brown.

Serve with jam and cream.

Note: If self-rising flour is not available, simply make your own by adding 2 teaspoons of baking powder for every 1 cup of all-purpose flour.

Easy Vanilla Slice

Vanilla Slices are an Aussie favourite, sold in bakeries across the country. This is a simplified version of an old classic.

2 sheets frozen puff pastry, thawed.
300 ml/ 1 1/4 cups milk
600 ml/ 2 1/2 cups thickened heavy cream
2 packets instant vanilla pudding mix
Icing/confectioner's sugar for dusting.

Preheat oven to 200 C (375 F). Line two trays with baking paper. Place a sheet of pastry on each tray, and use a fork to prick all over. Bake for 10 minutes or until golden brown. Leave to cool.

Line a square 25cm/ 10" slice pan with baking paper, extending paper at two of the sides.

Using an electric mixer, beat milk, cream and pudding mix in a large bowl until thick, smooth and creamy.

Place one sheet of puff pastry in the prepared tin, flat side down.

Carefully spread mixture over the pastry, leveling the top.

Place the remaining pastry sheet over the top, flat side up, and gently press down. Refrigerate overnight.

Lift the slice out of the tin, using a serrated knife, cut into squares. Dust tops with icing sugar and serve.

Kitty Penrod

Kitty Penrod lives in Frisco, Texas. She was married to her high school sweetheart and was a Home Economics teacher in Columbus, Ohio before having her four children. Shortly after their 43rd Wedding Anniversary, her beloved husband passed away. She has eight grandchildren who bring her many blessings and joy!

Baking, cooking, having tea parties, water aerobics and praying are her passions.

If you'd like, you can check out her blog:

https://www.kittyskozykitchen.com

Patriotic Strawberries

Ingredients

- 1 quart container of strawberries, rinsed and let dry on a paper towel, leaving the leafy part of the strawberry intact
- 1 8 ounce pkg. of cream cheese, softened
- 1/2 cup of powdered sugar
- 1/2 teaspoon of vanilla or almond extract (I used vanilla bean paste)
- blueberries for garnish or anything of your choosing

Instructions

1. Cream together the softened cream cheese with the powdered sugar and add the extract.
2. Cut an X on the pointed end of the strawberry, not cutting all the way down to the leafy part.
3. Using the star tip in a disposable piping bag, or using a food safe bag, with one of the ends cut off, fill the bag and close. Squeeze the filling into the top of the strawberry. I personally like a good amount! Top with a blueberry or any other garnish of your choosing.
4. These are best eaten the same day!

Sponge Cake

Ingredients

- 2 eggs, at room temperature
- 1/4 teaspoon salt
- 1 cup sugar
- 1 teaspoon vanilla
- 1/2 cup milk, boiling hot
- 1 tablespoon butter
- 1 cup flour
- 1 teaspoon baking powder

Instructions

1. Grease and flour a 9" cake pan, either round or square.
2. Preheat oven to 350 degrees.
3. Beat eggs until very light in color. While you're doing this, you can heat your milk and butter together in the microwave or in a saucepan, until boiling.
4. Beat in very well the salt, sugar and vanilla.
5. Slowly beat in the boiling hot milk and butter mixture.
6. Sift the flour and baking powder together in a bowl (I just whisk together), and beat into the egg mixture.
7. Pour very quickly into the prepared pan. Bake immediately for 25-30 minutes, or until the top of the cake springs back when lightly touched with your fingertip.

Oatmeal Cherry Cookies

Ingredients:
- 2 sticks butter, softened
- 1 cup sugar
- 1 cup brown sugar
- 2 eggs
- 1/2 t. vanilla
- 1/2 t. almond extract
- 2 cups flour
- 1 t. salt
- 1 t. baking soda
- 1 teaspoon cinnamon
- 1/4 teaspoon cardamom
- 3 cups oatmeal
- 2 cups dried cherries

Instructions:
1. Place the butter, brown sugar & sugar in the bowl of electric mixer, fitted with paddle attachment. Beat on medium speed for about 30 seconds., until the mixture is fluffy. Turn down the speed to low & add the eggs & the extracts. Beat for about 30 seconds longer.
2. In a mixing bowl, sift together the flour, baking soda ,salt, cinnamon and cardamom. Add to the mixer, while beating on low speed & beat for about 15 seconds, stopping the mixer once to scrape down the sides. Add the oatmeal & cherries & beat for about 15 seconds.
3. Using an ice cream scoop, scoop the dough & put onto parchment-lined baking sheets. Refrigerate the cookie balls on the sheets for about an hour. Gently press out the dough with the back of your hand. Bake at 350 degrees for 12-15 minutes. Makes about 30 cookies.

Pumpkin Roll

Ingredients

- For the cake:
- 3 eggs
- 3/4 cup sugar
- 1/4 cup firmly packed brown sugar
- 1 cup pumpkin (I always freeze the rest of the pumpkin for another recipe)
- 1 cup flour
- 1 teaspoon baking powder
- 1/2 teaspoon salt
- 1 teaspoon pumpkin pie spice
- 1 teaspoon cinnamon
- 1/4 teaspoon nutmeg
- 1 cup finely chopped pecans
- 2 tablespoons powdered sugar
- For the Filling:
- 1 (8-ounce) pkg. cream cheese, softened
- 1/4 cup butter, softened
- 1 and 1/4 cup powdered sugar
- 1 teaspoon vanilla

Instructions for the Cake:

1. Preheat oven to 375 degrees.
2. Grease an 15″ x 10″ jelly roll pan. Line with wax paper or parchment paper, and grease and flour that (I use a spray that contains flour.)
3. Combine eggs, and both sugars and beat on high speed of an electric mixer until smooth. Add pumpkin, mixing well.
4. Combine the flour, baking powder, salt and spices, stirring well; add to pumpkin mixture and mix until smooth.
5. Pour the batter into the prepared pan, and spread evenly, then sprinkle with pecans. Bake for 12-15 minutes, or until top of cake springs back when touched.
6. Sprinkle 2 tablespoons of powdered sugar evenly onto a tea towel. Loosen edges of cake and carefully invert onto towel. Remove the wax or parchment paper. Roll up cake in towel, beginning with short side. Cool cake completely on a cooling rack

For the Filling:

7. 1. Combine the butter and cream cheese in a medium bowl, and beat with and electric mixer until smooth. Add the powdered sugar and the vanilla and beat again until smooth.
8. 2. Carefully unroll cake and spread with cream cheese filling to within 1/2″ of edges. Carefully reroll cake without the towel. Place on a serving platter; chill before serving.

Bunny Cakelets

You can use this recipe to make vanilla or chocolate bunnies. I used a cream cheese frosting for the tails.

Ingredients
- 1 cup sugar
- 1/2 cup butter melted and slightly cooled
- 1 1/2 cups flour
- 1/2 cup milk
- 1 teaspoon baking powder
- 1 teaspoon vanilla
- 1/4 teaspoon salt
- 2 eggs
- 2 tablespoons cocoa (optional)

Instructions
1. Preheat oven to 350.
2. Prep pan with shortening and flour or use baking spray.
3. In a large bowl mix sugar and butter at low speed until well blended, then increase to medium speed and beat until light and fluffy.
4. Add flour, milk, baking powder, cocoa powder, vanilla, salt and eggs.
5. Pour evenly into prepared pans. Tap the pan on the counter to remove air bubbles.
6. Bake for 20-30 minutes or until toothpick inserted in the cake's center comes out clean.
7. Cool cake in pan on rack for 10 minutes. Turn out on rack and cool completely.

In Closing

We have now come to the close of the second book in A Southern Lady's tea book series. I hope you have enjoyed the short, but hopefully descriptive stories of my tea adventures in other countries!

I have learned so very much in being pressed in this direction of writing, not only this book, but the one that gave birth to this series of tea books, A Southern Lady's Tea Journey: A Legacy.

If you have not read the first in the series, I hope you will. It is another book of very short stories about my childhood and my ancestors, the founding fathers of New Orleans and Baton Rouge.

We are living in very dark days, and when I began to write these books, I wanted to bring something of beauty, light-heartedness, with a little whimsy, and happiness that could shift us away from the heaviness of our day.

There is a quote by a very famous American Jewish author and rabbi, Chaim Potok. He wrote, The Chosen and The Promise and several other books. He famously said:

"Come, let us have some tea and continue to talk about happy things!"

When we read this simple quote, we might think, "That's nice," but when we know the story behind the statement and why it became such a famous quote, we can understand its seriousness and why, sometimes, just having a cup of tea, either with a friend or alone, can truly be a soothing and comforting experience. Without going into a lot of detail, Rabbi Potok was writing about harsh circumstances that surrounded his people, who had been forced to live very differently than they were accustomed to.

He was born in 1929, the same year as my mother, who is now 92, and then grew up in the years following the Great Depression, when life was harsh and days were dark for so many. It took time to recover from those dark days.

It could have been during the Second World War, when life in Europe was dark and harsh situations and restrictions surrounded the Jewish people. Well, history has a way of repeating itself. But whatever the situation that causes us to be thrust into days we are not accustomed to that seem to be dark with harsh restrictions, in the midst of it all:

Come, let us have some tea, and we will talk about happy things!"

A Southern Lady's Tea Journey

A Legacy

Andrea "Andy" McDougal

The First in the Tea Book Series:

A Southern Lady's Tea Journey

Order your copy today from

Amazon or Barnes & Noble

or get an autographed copy from

the author at:

tea.garden.publications@gmail.com

See the next page for her other books

Other Books
by Andrea "Andy" McDougal

The Glory of God Revealed

His Wonders in the Deep

Your Camels Are Coming

Understanding the Seed

The Arrows of the Lord

The Power of the Seed

Author Contact

I welcome your comments and suggestions.

andysministry@gmail.com

Tea.Garden.Publications@gmail.com

Phone: 225-572-9844

www.facebook.com/andrea.mcdougal.3

www.facebook.com/andymcdougalministries

www.instagram/andrea.mcdougal.3

www.instagram/asouthernladysteas

Words by A.A. Milne for Winnie the Pooh that I could not
leave out of this book, words from the heart of a genius.

If there ever comes a day
When we can't be together,
Keep me in your heart.
I'll stay there forever.

A day without a friend
is like a pot
without a single drop of honey left inside.

If you live to be a hundred,
I want to live to be a hundred minus one day
so I never have to live without you.

How lucky I am to have
something that makes saying goodbye so hard.

Any day spent with you is my Favorite Day.
So, today is my New Favorite Day.

"Pooh?" whispered Piglet.
"Yes, Piglet?" said Pooh.
"Oh, nothing," said Piglet.
"I was just making sure of you."

If ever there is a tomorrow
When we are not together,
There is something you must always remember.
You are braver than you believe,
Stronger that you seem,
And smarter that you think.
But the most important thing is:
Even if we are apart...
I'll always be with you!

Bibliography

......., *The Afternoon Tea Collection*, 2012, New York, New York, Sterling Publishing

Barnes, Emilie, *An Invitation to Tea: Special Celebrations with Treasured Friends*, 1996, Eugene, Oregon, Harvest House Publishers

Blake, Susannah, *Afternoon Tea*, 2006, New York, New York, Ryland Peters & Small

Calvert, Catherine, *Having Tea: Recipes & Table Settings by Tricia Folley*, 1987, New York, New York, Clarkson N. Potter, Inc.

Ellis, Alda, *Southern Teatime Pleasures: Simple Ideas and Recipes*, 2012, Eugene, Oregon, Harvest House Publishers

Engelbreit, Mary, *Time for Tea: A Book about Tea*, 1997, Kansas City, Missouri Andrews McMeel Publishing

Fraser, Linda (senior editor), *The Perfect Afternoon Tea Book: A Collection of Teatime Treats*, 1997, New York, New York, Lorenz Books

Heiss, Mary Lou and Robert J, *The Story of Tea: A Cultural History and Drinking Guide*, 2007, Berkeley, California, Ten Speed Books

Johnson, Margaret, *Tea & Crumpets: Recipes & Rituals from European Tearooms & Cafes*, 2009, San Francisco, California, Chronicle Books LLC.

Manchester, Carole, French Tea: The Pleasures of the Table, 1993, New York, New York, Hearst Books

Marcus, Bonnie, Guilt-Free Girl DessertsL Delicious Figure-Friendly Recipes for Any Occasion, 2013, New York, Newq York, Parragon Inc.

Reeves, Lorna (editor), *The Ultimate TeaTime Collection: Scones, Savories and Sweets*, 2018, Birmingham, Alabama, hm books, Hoffman Media, LLC

Richardson, Bruce, *The Great Tea Rooms of Britain,* 1997, Perryville, Kentucky, Benjamin Press

Richardson, Bruce, *The Great Tea Rooms of America*, 2002, Perryville, Kentucky, Benjamin Press

Simson, Helen, *The London Ritz Book of Afternoon Tea*, 1986, New York, New York, William Morrow

Waller, Kim, *The Essential Tea Companion,* 2009, New York, New York, Hearst Books

Waller, Kim, *The Art of Taking Tea*, 2002, New York, New York, Hearst Books

Waller, Kim, *The Pleasures of Tea: Recipes & Rituals*, 1999, New York, New York, Hearst Books

Wong, Alice (editor), *The Charms of Tea: Reminiscences and Recipes,* 1991, New York, New York, Hearst Books

www.ingramcontent.com/pod-product-compliance
Lightning Source LLC
Chambersburg PA
CBHW041537120626
46551CB00019B/2726